Mary
Our Hope

Mary
Our Hope

A Selection from the
Sermons, Addresses, and Papers
of

Cardinal John J. Wright

Prepared and Edited by
R. Stephen Almagno, O.F.M.

RESONARE CHRISTUM

Ignatius Press   San Francisco

Imprimi Potest:	Alban V. Montella, O.F.M.
	Minister Provincial
	Provincial Curia
	New York City
Imprimatur:	+ John R. Quinn
	Archbishop of San Francisco

Cover by Victoria Hoke Lane

All royalty proceeds accruing to the editor from the sale of this book
will be paid to the Catholic Institute of Pittsburgh, Inc., for works of
religion, charity, and education.

To

Cardinal John J. Wright
1909–1979

In

Loyalty and Gratitude

Publication of this book was made possible by the generous donations of Mr. Thomas J. Donnelly, Mrs. Frederick N. Egler, and Mr. C. Holmes Wolfe, Jr., Trustees of the Mary J. Donnelly Foundation.

Tribute to Cardinal Wright

It would be impossible for me not to recall for you, here present, who diligently follow the events of the universal Church, the wonderful figure of Cardinal John Joseph Wright, Prefect of the Sacred Congregation for the Clergy, whom the Lord called to Himself on Friday last, August 10, 1979. He has thus crowned with a holy death an existence which was spent totally for Christ and for the Church. As a priest, as a bishop in the United States of America, as a cardinal in charge of an important department of the Roman Curia, he was always faithful to his motto: *Resonare Christum corde Romano*. That really sums up his whole life. In fact, Cardinal Wright was a secure voice which preached Our Lord with a fidelity and a directness which arose from a *sensus Ecclesiae* which was second nature to him.

Everyone who knew Cardinal Wright had to love him because hidden beneath his humorous character was a singular clarity of ideas, goodness, and kindness.

All of us confidently hope that the Lord has set aside for him the destiny of the Just. It is for this that we pray, confiding his immortal soul to the maternal intercession of the Virgin, assumed into heaven.[1]

Pope John Paul II

Contents

Preface

Sometime during 1976, Cardinal Wright expressed, to Father Wuerl and me, the hope of publishing (in separate, convenient, and inexpensive editions) some of his sermons and writings on Our Lady, the saints, and other matters to which he had devoted his heart, mind, pen, and voice. At that time, Father Wuerl and I actually began working with the Cardinal on such a project. But, due to his duties as Prefect of the Sacred Congregation for the Clergy, the demands made on him by the various Vatican congregations and commissions of which he was an active member, and the increasing advance of the illness that was to cause his death, the Cardinal was obliged to husband his time and energies. The hope of publishing some of his sermons, addresses, and papers—together with the intention of writing his autobiography—was put aside to another day. Alas, that day never came.

Four years later, on July 24, 1980, when the executors of Cardinal Wright's will appointed me to serve as the literary executor of his estate, I told them—remembering the Cardinal's wishes—that besides preparing for publication a main collection of Wright's sermons, addresses, and papers, I intended, also, to edit several smaller volumes on Our Lady, the saints, and other matters. This volume, *Mary Our Hope*, is a selection—covering twenty-seven years (1948–1975)—from some of the sermons, addresses, and papers wherein Cardinal Wright reflected on Our Lady.

In publishing these texts I hope, as Bishop Anthony G. Bosco has written in his introduction to vol. II (*The Pittsburgh Years: 1959–1969*) of *Resonare Christum: A Selection from the Sermons, Addresses, and Papers of Cardinal John J. Wright*, that "those of us who heard many of them delivered will now in the reading hear reecho in our minds and hearts and souls the accents of the *Yankee Bishop of Pittsburgh*, the universal churchman, the man who taught us what being all things to all men really means. We will hear again the echo of his voice and be reminded of the depth of his thought, the joy of his wit, the sound of his laughter, his love for Christ and the Church, his compassion for people."

Moreover, with Bishop Bosco, "I hope that those who did not know John Wright and those who never met him will meet the man in his sermons, addresses, and papers. For his talks were the man, and the man was his talks. Read the talks, and you meet John Wright. Read the talks, and you will know his concerns, the things he cared about, the things that mattered to him. Read the talks, and you will know that he was always concerned about the things of God and mankind. I hope that you, too, will pick up the echo of his laughter and the depth of his person."

Mindful of the Cardinal's days in this city, as well as his concern for and involvement in the academic life of this university, Chancellor Wesley W. Posvar, Ph.D., and Dean Thomas J. Galvin, Ph.D., of the University of Pittsburgh—where I have the privilege to work and lecture in such congenial surroundings—have both been most cooperative with anything and everything that has concerned the publication of Cardinal Wright's papers.

Miss JoAnn Hartz, my secretary, Miss Audrey Daigneault, my graduate student assistant, and Miss Melody Mazuk have also been most helpful and cooperative. To each of these persons, to Dr. Ellen G. Detlefsen, and to my colleagues here at the university, my very sincere gratitude.

Ever since my coming to the University of Pittsburgh, the Diocese of Pittsburgh, and in particular the Very Reverend Leo V. Vanyo, J.C.D., has afforded me both the hospitality of the Cathedral Parish House and the opportunity to serve the parishioners of Saint Paul Cathedral. Thus, as was the case with Cardinal Wright, this New Englander has come to know and love the people of Pittsburgh.

Finally, I am grateful to the Reverend Alban V. Montella, O.F.M., my Minister Provincial, for his constant encouragement and support.

R. Stephen Almagno, O.F.M.
The University of Pittsburgh
School of Library and Information Science
April 10, 1984

Acknowledgments

The literary executor is grateful to the following for permission to reproduce copyright material:

The Annals of Saint Anthony's Shrine for "Mary and Modern Times" and "Mary and Christian Unity".

The Catholic University of America Press (*American Ecclesiastical Review*) for "Some Street Shrines of Rome" and "Pastoral Letter on the Dogma of the Assumption".

The Reverend Brendan Keevey, C.P., Provincial (*Sign*) for "Lourdes, Land of the Rosary".

L'Osservatore Romano, English language edition, for "The Cult of Mary in the Age of the Cult of the Flesh", "Mary the New Eve", "Mary, Type of Servant and Agent of the Holy Spirit", and "Tribute to Cardinal Wright by Pope John Paul II".

Marian Era for "Our Lady of Space".

The Marianist for "Mary and Christian Unity" and "Why a Mexican Theme Issue?"

Marian Studies for "Mariology in the English-Speaking World", "Our Lady of Guadalupe", and "Memorial Tribute to Cardinal John Wright".

Marist Missions for "Our Lady of Space".

Our Lady's Digest for "Our Lady of Space" and "Mary the New Eve".

Prow Books (Franciscan Marytown Press) for "The Cult of Mary in the Age of the Cult of the Flesh".

The Thomist for "Mary Immaculate, Patroness of the United States".

Introduction

Though it may sound like something snipped out of a second nocturn in the old Breviary, it is a fact that John Wright was developing a devotion to Our Blessed Mother even back in his boyhood days. Every Wednesday afternoon, he hiked up the hill from Boston Latin School to the tall twin spires and booming bells of the Mission Church, trooping along with the throng gathered for the novena in honor of Our Mother of Perpetual Help.[1]

The years rolled on, the Mission Church became a basilica, and the young student became Cardinal John Wright.[2] In 1974—if I may intrude the personal—he did me the great honor of preaching there at my Golden Jubilee as a Redemptorist.[3] By that time arthritis had begun its crippling work on his overburdened legs, so I gently hinted that he deliver his homily from the lectern on the floor of the sanctuary instead of climbing the high marble pulpit. His response was almost a glare: "I'll preach from that pulpit if it is the last thing I do!" And he did, with the usual masterly flow of phrase and the trembling fire which were his trademark.

On that occasion he shook his head sadly over how the neighborhood around the church had changed. Thereafter, whenever he wrote me here he would scrawl at the bottom of the stately formal Vatican envelope in his own bold, black handwriting: "Opposite Funeral Parlor".

In part this was an allusion to the fact that I have lived in the same room with the same somber view for forty-three years. I never told him that the boarded-up

17

drug store next to the funeral parlor had been the scene of a double murder and that in the pie-shop next to that the baker had got a bullet in the belly. No wonder the crowds stopped coming to the basilica.

But the neighborhood around Boston's majestic cathedral in another part of town has changed too, and that reminds me of a day when Father Wright stole the show in the cathedral without opening his mouth. The occasion was the Funeral Mass of Cardinal O'Connell who could give the Boston Brahmins lessons in lofty manners. When he died, Father Wright was his secretary.[4] At the lordly obsequies, down the long cathedral aisle marched a sizeable part of the national hierarchy: monsignori, bishops, archbishops, cardinals—a gorgeous pageant of flowing purples and scarlets and crimsons, like a slowly moving sunset. And in the midst of it, almost like a fly on a stained-glass window, one priest processed in a simple black cassock with a light Roman cape billowing behind him. In his outstretched hands Father Wright carried the letter of condolence from the Pope. Everybody was wondering who was that sole bit of black in the huge red sea.

Somehow that recalls, not a procession, but a parade. That was Boston's biggest demonstration in honor of the Holy Name, a spectacle like the American Legion Parade, tramping on for hours upon hours. The formal attire of a bishop in those undemocratic days was silk hat and morning coat, and the recently ordained Bishop Wright swung along in the front rank, waving an arm of recognition right and left, flashing his eyes like a young Italian prince, a genuine specimen of the dark Irish.

In those days his personal architecture was slimly Gothic, before the inexorable years turned it into rotund

Romanesque. Far from a towering presence, he favored the squat French mitre rather than the monumental beehive preferred by many bishops. This may have been influenced by his first years in the priesthood when he spent his university vacations as a curate in a tiny French village.[5] Or was he a Francophile because of his long-standing interest in Saint Joan of Arc? Certainly he had amassed the most complete collection on Saint Joan in this country, an incredible array of volumes now lining the shelves of the Cheverus Room in the Boston Public Library.[6] The prelate after whom the room is named was Boston's first Catholic bishop, and if anyone doubts that he was French, let me list the litany of his names: Jean Louis Anne Madeleine Lefebvre de Cheverus. May one doubt that the Indians for whom he worked in the Maine woods ever called him all that?

John Wright was a much simpler handle, and in so many ways he was a simple man: simple in the sense of unaffected. As a cardinal, resident in Rome and head of a Vatican congregation—the one in charge of all the Catholic clergy throughout the world—he wore the crimson robes of his office when ceremony or protocol demanded it but otherwise confined himself to unpretentious black. I recall him in a plain black cassock guiding me in my American black suit through the streets of Rome to a restaurant. "No tourist trap, here!" he boasted. "No American has been in this place for twenty years." Then he and the waiter put on a pleasant act, arguing up and down the menu about just what to order. It was all like a scene from an opera, and it made me remember that the Cardinal had captained his debating team at Boston Latin and Boston College.[7]

Debater he was; athlete, never. Call him the ultimate

intellectual for whom sports did not exist. Like the old priest in the film, *Going My Way*, he would not know which end of a caddy to hold. He used to say with a wry smile that if ever he should get the notion to exercise, he would banish it like a bad thought. This is a pity because more activity would have meant less weight, and weight, I suspect, was one of the grim factors that did him in at the end.

Some priests play tennis; some play golf. Some fish and some ski. As priest, bishop, and cardinal, John Wright hardly walked. You could not even say about him, as you can say about many, that he walked only as far as his car, because he did not even drive. The car picked him up. What he did do was run up and down columns of print, and it was an exception if his bed lamp clicked off before two in the morning. The day was for working and the night was for reading; or more precisely, for studying, because his literary fare was never frothy snow-pudding but solid and even heavy stuff, with theology and history as the main courses.

Into this deep well of knowledge he dropped the bucket of an insatiably curious mind and brought up the material for his lectures and sermons. All his life he had far more speaking requests than he could ever honor. Yet, for a tremendously popular preacher, he did not have the deep, rich voice that rolls out glorious tones like a cathedral organ. On the contrary, his timber tended to be thin and pitched a bit high, but you forgot all that in his dynamic projection. Far from a monotonous, level, railroad-track delivery, he had the curves and dips, the unexpected rises and swoops, of a roller coaster. By lingering on a word, he could drop over it like an ermine cape that gave it an importance it normally never had. He would hit an emphatic phrase with the crispness of a hammer. His was the unconscious art of the born actor, blended with the conviction of the dedicated apostle. It came out as the really rare orator who taught you, persuaded you, moved you.

Incidentally, one of his chief weapons was wit. Light-hearted humor laced his serious messages like playful whitecaps on a deep sea. He loved to laugh.

Beneath all this lay, of course, the strong, solid foundation of the spiritual. Without it, the rest—in him or in any of us—is mere crepe paper. *Resonare Christum!* This he chose as the motto for his coat of arms. "To Reecho Christ!"[8] A completely involved churchman with no outside interests whatever, he lived entirely for God and for the spread of the kingdom. Even the Vatican has to have its bureaucracy, and Cardinal Wright administered one of those bureaus—the Sacred Congregation for the Clergy—but he never let the desk loom so large that it blotted out the prie-dieu or the altar. God, not government—even ecclesiastical—always came first. Many a time he came away from a high-level think-tank at the Vatican to head for a period of prayer at some shrine of Our Lady. A greybeard in wisdom, he was childlike in his simple, unassuming piety.

On Sunday afternoons he loved to take a ride through the Roman countryside, eventually reaching some spot dedicated to the Madonna. More often than not his ride took him along the Appian Way to the shrine of *La Madonna del Divino Amore*. Another favorite destination, in the town of Genezzano, was the chapel with the famous painting of Our Lady of Good Counsel. If the

Cardinal had brought some priest along for the ride, he would first point to the plaque that said: "Pope Pius IX made a pilgrimage to this Marian shrine prior to the opening of Vatican Council I." Then the Cardinal would stride to the opposite wall and read aloud the other plaque: "Pope John XXIII visited this shrine prior to the opening of Vatican Council II." Then the Cardinal would whirl around and say with darting eyes: "I wonder how many of those who speak equivocally about 'the spirit of Vatican II' are aware that it started here?"

As a newly ordained priest—Mary was never far from his priesthood—he said his second Mass at the Roman shrine of *La Madonna della Strada*, but his very first Mass was touching enough to be in honor of Mary, Comfortress of the Afflicted. In a letter to his parents, written that week, he says:

No one pays much attention to blind kids, and their asylum here is a bleak enough place—so I thought I'd find it inspiring for me and perhaps a little pleasure for them if I celebrated my First Mass among them and for them. I at least received *my part* of that hope! The Mass was at 6:30 A.M. with a choir of blind boys singing and a blind boy at the organ. The children—sixty boys and thirty girls— received Holy Communion, and as long as I live I shall have in my eyes the sight of those blind kids kneeling at the altar. It was too grand to be saddening. No thrill you can imagine could equal mine when I had the privilege of placing the Host on the tongues of those splendid sons and daughters of God, while asking Christ to keep them close to Him and bring them to life everlasting. After Mass I sat on a great chair before the high altar and each boy and girl was led forward for my first blessing. Many of them would smile and say: "Thank you"—so grateful for the tiniest recognition are these youngsters.

This somehow resurrects the memory of something Cardinal Wright said about the Boy, Jesus. You have to realize that perhaps because he had once taught theology, he had small patience with pretentious new theories that were as far out as satellites from the old doctrines. He felt an almost personal grief that, as he phrased it, "the clear fixed stars of the Catholic faith are momentarily obscured by theological smog." Someone once asked him what he thought of the recent theory that it dawned on Christ only gradually that He was the Son of God. Cardinal Wright answered with withering sarcasm: "I can see it all so plainly. The twelve-year-old Boy bursts into the kitchen at Nazareth, the screen door slamming behind Him, and He runs up to His Mother and bursts out, 'Gee, Mom, guess *what!* "

As his favorite Marian shrine was Lourdes, his favorite Marian devotion was the rosary. He was wont to wrinkle a disapproving nose at the mention of a wake service that featured a few verses of Scripture and a couple of sentimental poems. He liked to point out that the greater part of the rosary was scooped right out of the Scriptures and that most funeral-parlor poetry was pious fluff. "When I am laid out," he would say, "start the beads. And if no one has a pair, look in my pocket. They will be there, unless the undertaker has taken them out."

I wonder how many times he was part of the candle-lit Rosary Procession at Lourdes? Once he invited me to be his guest on the *White Train*. At that time all I knew was that the *White Train* was in some manner connected with

23

Lourdes. I learned the hard way and loved it. It was called the *White Train* because of the white banners slung along the sides, but more so because of the white uniforms of the dozens of doctors and nurses aboard. It was an annual trip that carried about three hundred and fifty sick priests who were brought from all over Italy to a railway yard in Rome for a pilgrimage to Lourdes.

Blind priests, crippled priests, cancer-ridden priests, in a word, priests with all manner of diseases filled the long train. We did not take off our clothes in the whole thirty-hour trip, but who could complain when you saw such helplessness all around you? At each of the half-dozen stations where we stopped, the priests and people of the town were there with food. (We had set out with nothing!) While the pasta and fruit and salami and the rest were taken aboard, Cardinal Wright was on the platform, bullhorn in hand, addressing the crowd. As he spoke, they laughed, they applauded, they blinked back tears: They were in the palm of his hand. Admiration and affection sparkled in their eyes. By the last stop, though, he was hoarse and limp.

Around the parklike grounds of Lourdes, you would come upon the Cardinal pulling a wheelchair or pushing a rolling stretcher bed. On the last morning he was the chief celebrant at the farewell Mass. Like the Last Supper, there were twelve bishops around the altar. Like Pentecost, the readings, very brief, were in five different languages. And, like the sick who came to Christ in Galilee, there were three hundred and fifty sick priests in rows upon rows of wheelchairs, bright stoles over their bathrobes, concelebrating. As many more of us who were healthy —perhaps seven hundred in all—said our part of the

Mass from the pews. Cardinal Wright never seemed more the head of the Sacred Congregation for the Clergy of the world than in that sacred hour.[9]

Now, in a final sense, his own pilgrimage as a sick priest is over and he has reached home. At last he is with the Lady he loved and the Lord he served.

But for many of us his memory lingers on.

Joseph E. Manton, C.SS.R.

Basilica of Our Lady of Perpetual Help
The Mission Church
Boston, Massachusetts

I

Our Lady of the Snow

The classic pattern of the homily requires that we seek the inspiration of our thought in the words of the day's liturgy. But, in order to lift your thoughts to her for whose Votive Mass we gather, let me recall first the pious legend which is commemorated by the feast we celebrate: the dedication of the Church of Our Lady of the Snow.

The church, whose foundation today rejoices us, is the glorious basilica of Saint Mary Major in Rome. It is perhaps the largest, in many ways the noblest, of all temples dedicated to the Blessed Mother of God. Some claim it to be the first publicly consecrated to Our Lady in that city of Rome whence the vicar of her Son rules the Universal Catholic Church. Its accumulated dignities account for the name *Saint Mary Major*, but quite as ancient, among the Roman people, is the title attached to it by popular devotion and by today's liturgy: the church of Our Lady of the Snow.

In the days of Pope Liberius, who ruled the Church of God from the year 352 until his death in 366, there lived in Rome a man named John who owned a farmland on the Esquiline Hill. John and his wife loved God, but the joy of their virtuous life together was overshadowed by the sadness of entering old age without son or daughter to whom they might transmit their honored name, their

This sermon was preached in Boston, Massachusetts, on August 5, 1948.

temporal possessions, and the piety of their faith. Inspired by the latter, they resolved to make Our Lady heiress of all their property, and they asked of her some sign by which her good pleasure might be made known to them. One night John lay dreaming, and as he slept a voice from on high bade him give to the Holy Father that portion of their land which they would find blanketed in snow on the following morning. Today, we commemorate the events of that morning, August 5, 358, when the devout John found a mantle of snow on the slopes of his farm. John instantly sought out the Holy Father and found that Pope Liberius had similarly received an inspiration from heaven which had commanded him to build on land which would be white with snow a great church to the honor of the Virgin Mother of God whose spotless purity a miracle would symbolize. And so that morning in August, the hottest month in all the Roman year, the Holy Father traced in the heaven-sent snow the outlines of the glorious church which stands to this day in tribute to the purity of Our Blessed Lady.

Should we not pause to ask ourselves why this greatest of all churches dedicated to Mary, this most ancient of the existing temples reared in her honor and most privileged of basilicas bearing her name, commemorates the mystery of her purity? Of all the attributes of Mary her purity seems most to fascinate our minds and fire our hearts. Why? Why does her purity preoccupy us so? We are a race, we humans, enamored of beauty. Mary is the *Mother Most Amiable*, the *Mother Most Admirable*, the *Mystical Rose*, the *House of Gold*, the *Morning Star*—but few temples have been reared, by us who love beauty, to celebrate these fair attributes of the most beautiful of all the King's daughters. Why is it always her *purity* to which our thoughts are turned? We are a people awed by wisdom. Mary is the *Virgin Most Prudent*, the *Seat of Wisdom*, the *Queen of the Patriarchs*, *Prophets*, and *Apostles* —but few, indeed, are the great shrines dedicated to these venerable qualities. We are prone to cultivate fame and those who possess it. Mary is the *Virgin Most Renowned*, the *Vessel of Honor*, of *Singular Devotion*, the *Queen of All Saints*—yet no common instinct impels us to hail her under these proud titles of acclaim. We are a nation avid for power. Mary is the *Virgin Most Powerful*, the *Tower of David*, the *Strength of the Weak*, the *Help of Christians*; the liturgy speaks of her as being of strength, a strength commanding like that to an army, unconquerable and compact—and yet, save in the time of affliction and of great need, we do not seem to pay tribute to Mary in terms of her power. Always we are preoccupied by her *purity*. Of all her attributes this most haunts us; of all her qualities this most causes us to hush, to bow our heads in prayer, alike of petition and of praise. *Mother Most Pure!* So under every sky the believing breathe to her their love and need. *Ave Maria*—undefiled! *Ave Maria*—stainless styled! So even the unbelieving cry. *Mother Fairest*, *Mother Purest*, *Virgin Most Pure*—this the constant song of those who love her most.[1]

Why does her purity so preoccupy our minds, so silence our speech, so inflame our hearts? Perhaps it is because in no wise are we so pathetically alien to her. Wisdom we have in part; knowledge—alas! sometimes we are surfeited with it. Power we have of a kind; and fame is the food on which we grow fat. With all her other qualities, we can make some show of kinship. But the most strong, the most wise, the most fair, the most renowned of us must bow our heads whenever there is mention of the *purity* of the Mother of God!

The liturgy, quite as much as popular lore or the poet's

song, proclaims her purity. Theology unravels all implications in propositions which admit of no debate. But that same theology reminds us at every turn of our impurity, our tainted nature. And if the poets have best sung her purity, a poet, too, most accurately confessed our confusion:

> Dark Angel, with thine aching lust
> To rid the world of penitence:
> Malicious Angel, who still dost
> My soul such sublime violence!
>
> Because of thee, no thought, no thing,
> Abides for me undesecrate:
> Dark Angel, ever on wing,
> Who never reachest me too late!
>
> When music sounds, then changest thou
> Its silvery to a sultry fire:
> Nor will thine envious heart allow
> Delight untortured by desire.
>
> Through thee, the gracious Muses turn
> To Furies, O mine Enemy!
> And all the things of beauty burn
> With flames of evil ecstasy.
>
> Because of thee, the land of dreams
> Becomes a gathering place of fears:
> Until tormented slumber seems
> Our vehemence of useless tears.
>
> When sunlight glows upon the flowers,
> Or ripples down the dancing sea:

Thou, with thy troop of passionate powers,
Beleaguerest, bewilderest, me.

Within the breath of autumn woods,
Within the winter silences:
Thy venomous spirit stirs and broods,
O Master of impieties!

The ardour of red flame is thine,
And thine the steely soul of ice:
Thou poisonest the fair design
Of nature, with unfair device.

Apples of ashes, golden bright;
Water of bitterness, how sweet!
O banqueting of foul delight,
Prepared by thee, dark Paraclete![2]

Save only Mary, every child of Adam knows full well the meaning of these lines. Out of our knowledge comes the prayer, pathetic and sincere, with which we hail her purity.

The chasm between Mary and ourselves created by her singular purity and our defilement finds her alone on one side and all humankind—without exception—on the other. Even the greatest of our saints, save only Mary, at one time or another have been averted from God: be this said unto our consolation. Indeed, as the eagle-preacher reminds us, Christ entrusted the highest offices within His gift to sinners. The supreme charge over His flock He gave to Peter who denied Him. The first of His evangelists was the Publican, Matthew. The favored watcher at His Cross, the first recipient of His Easter blessing, was the Magdalen. The foremost of His preachers was Paul, who persecuted the Church of God and who acknowledges on his every page his guilt before God and men. So has it been in the history of His Church ever since. Not the just and innocent but converted sinners are typically chosen to serve Him. All those closest to Him—save only Mary, His Mother—were from among them. She alone was conceived holy in the sight of God, cleansed from before her conception, immaculate and pure from the first primeval moment when God Himself first thought of her.

Again, why? Christ chose penitent sinners, even for high places in His apostolate. There are literally none among all mankind, not even saints, who are not penitents. He did not call into being a special breed of men to be His priests and prophets and co-workers because in one subtle sense, a sense of which the Holy Saturday Liturgy so beautifully reminds us, it was *better*, so to say, that those who would be His apostles be themselves sinners.[3] He chose them *for others*, Bossuet reminds us; He chose Mary for *Himself*! He chose those whom He would send to others from among sinners in order that they might the more persuasively announce His mercy and the better understand the pathos of our sin. His whole plan of redemption required that He restore confidence to souls discouraged by guilt, that He give *true* peace of mind to lives disordered by sin. Therefore He chose penitent men rather than angels to be the preachers of His gospel: For who could better preach the Divine Mercy than those who personally tasted it: those who could say with Saint Paul that *Christ came into this world to save sinners . . . yes, sinners, . . . sinners of whom I am the chief*.

But for Himself the God in Christ could fashion only an extraordinary being of privileged purity. Those who would be the human channels of the life of our souls He would providentially choose from among the defiled, but she who would be the channel of *His own* humanity must have a purity somehow in conformity with the purity of Himself. Two loves were destined to be blended in the heart of Mary: She was to give her Son the love due to God, and her God the love due to a son. The love for her Son would be an impulse of nature; the love of her God an impulse of grace. And just as her Son was one with her God, so nature and grace, the two loves in Mary, unlike, alas, those which war in us, were intimately blended, and grace was present from the first moment that nature existed in her: Both were united in the single love of her Most Pure Heart.

Sinners are chosen to be our apostles because we ourselves are sinners. Mary was conceived and created spotless because the flesh which was to come from her own flesh must mirror the purity of the God who would wear it.

We who profess the ancient Christian faith concerning Mary and who cherish her with a special love inspired by that faith know all these things, yet we are not forgetful of the source of her perfection. Perfectly as Mary's innocence foreshadowed that of Christ, it was, as we well know, entirely different from His. Christ was all pure by a perfection that was His by right; Mary was pure by privilege of her office. Christ was total purity itself; Mary was purity totally bestowed. Christ was sinless by nature, Mary by grace, by God's favor. In Christ we adore the very source of innocence; in Mary we admire the perfect reflection of its power. Christ wins for us by His purity our sanctification, the means to our cleansing. Mary exemplifies, in her purity, the possibilities of our poor flesh when God *is all and in all*. Mary, full of grace, bearing the Lord among us, is *blessed* among women—but she is still a woman, still flesh of our flesh, yet a pledge of what we may become in some degree through cooperation with the grace allotted to us whenever we, too, receive the Lord within us.

There are few among us so defiled but what the thought of Mary's purity serves to inspire us, to lift not merely our eyes but our very selves to the heaven which produced and received her most pure flesh. We all become the things we love. The love of earthly things makes us earthly. The love of vile things degrades and makes us vile. The love of heavenly things makes us somehow divine. The love of Mary makes us pure.

My dear brethren, here is the strangest paradox in all God's spiritual world: The purity of Mary fascinates us because we are ourselves so sinful and because by her purity she is lifted immeasurably apart from us. But the purity of Mary does not dismay or drive us from her. Great innocence of life in other human beings sometimes is a reproach to those who have lost their innocence; it seems to reprove, even to repel, the guilty. But the purity of Mary, by divine ingenuity, does not seem to reproach us to flight. We instinctively recognize that it exists to be our solace and salvation. It is because of her purity—strange and yet consoling paradox—that we who are defiled see in her, not the portent of our punishment, but the pledge of our own purification. It is sinners, not saints confirmed in grace, who cry out, "our life, our sweetness, and our hope" so confidently to the spotless Virgin, miraculous in her purity, among us as Christmas snows in Roman summer.

O Holy Virgin, in the midst of the joys of heaven, do not forget the sadness of the earth. Look with kindness on those who suffer, who are so bewildered by difficulties, who are scarred and stained by the sins of this life. Have pity on those who love but are separated. Have pity on the loneliness of our hearts. Have pity on the objects of our tenderness. Have pity on those who weep, on those who pray, on those who fear.

Mother Most Pure, give us peace. *Amen*.

II

Pastoral Letter on the
Dogma of the Assumption

During these recent days the Catholic world has devoutly anticipated and finally welcomed the solemn definition by our Holy Father, the Pope, of the dogma of the Assumption—that is, that Mary, the Virgin Mother of God, was assumed, body and soul, into the glory of heaven.

This historic definition has been an occasion of worldwide joy to the Church. It is welcomed with particular happiness here in the new Diocese of Worcester. Our diocese was created in this same Holy Year which has seen the fulfillment of the hopes of all who love Mary, the Mother of Christ.[1] Within our diocese is the only American college that takes its name from the Assumption of the Blessed Mother; it is staffed by the Assumption Fathers, who next month celebrate the centennial of their foundation.

Then, too, the Diocese of Worcester seems to have prepared especially for this great Marian definition. A principal popular devotion of our diocese has been the radio recitation of the rosary, a singularly beautiful devotion by means of which our homes, rectories,

This pastoral letter on the definition of the dogma of the Assumption, written on November 1, 1950, was addressed to the clergy, religious, and laity of the Diocese of Worcester, Massachusetts.

convents, and institutions throughout the diocese are brought together in a most intimate and prayerful unity. At regular intervals the whole diocese joins in collective, public meditation on the fourth of the glorious mysteries: the Assumption of the Blessed Mother into heaven.[2]

Hence, the particular fervor with which we join Catholics everywhere in hailing the honor paid the Queen of Christendom by this solemn declaration of the Catholic faith concerning Mary's death and assumption.

The dogmas which we Catholics believe are truths which have been revealed by God and handed down from the days when the Apostles first began to formulate, by authority of Our Lord Jesus Christ and under the guidance of the Holy Spirit, the statements of revealed truth which comprise the Catholic creed. Some of these truths we find in Sacred Scripture and believe on the authority of God when the Church proposes them to us as divinely revealed. Other truths, not found in Sacred Scripture, are taught to us by Christ's vicar, by Church councils, or by other established channels of divine teaching; these we also believe on the authority of God Who placed them in the deposit of faith originally entrusted to the Church and preserved in her Tradition.

The dogma of the Assumption is a dramatic example of a doctrine which the faithful themselves have transmitted in the Church since the days of the Apostles, always under the infallible guidance of the Church. The testimony of Scripture to this doctrine is in symbols and prophecies; it is not explicit. Neither has the solemn teaching authority of the Church hitherto dogmatically required explicit belief in the Assumption as it is now defined. Yet in all the history of the Church, always and everywhere in Christendom, the Catholic people by writings and words, by practices and prayers, have borne unanimous witness to their conviction that the body of the Blessed Mother never knew corruption; that after her death Jesus called her incorrupt into the company of Himself, her Son; of the Eternal Father, Whose perfect servant she is; and of all the saints, for she is their Queen.

To this constant Catholic belief concerning Mary's Assumption, the Holy Father has added new and powerful motives as a result of his dogmatic definition. The belief itself, however, remains unchanged; nothing has been added to it but clarity and the precision of definition. The Catholic faith concerning Mary has been confirmed, not changed; it is defined, not altered.

From the beginning Christians have believed the doctrine of Mary's Assumption, not merely because they know the Bible nor only because they accept the authority of the teaching Church; they have cherished this belief because they also know the human heart. In the understanding of the dogma of the Assumption the human heart sheds warm light on the deposit of faith.

A schoolmaster once remarked that he had one ultimate test by which to judge the basic goodness of a man. This test, he asserted, is valid however rich or poor a man may be and no matter what his other circumstances. It is the test of how he treats his own mother, with what gratitude he repays her goodness to him.

Most people will agree with the validity of that test. It prescinds from any question of a man's race, achievements, or class. The last quality, humanly speaking at least, which will desert any man still fundamentally sound in character is the quality of devotion to the one who gave him his flesh and blood, the breath of his life. The world retains a spot of sympathy for any man, however out-lawed, who in his moment of disgrace reveals a loving reverence for his mother. Conversely, the world rates none more despicable than the man, however renowned otherwise, who repudiates the mother who gave him birth.

Examples of the filial devotion of the truly great are many and touching. Few men in American history are more admired for their integrity and humanity than Abraham Lincoln. In many ways Lincoln was a rude man; he no doubt possessed his full measure of imper-fections. But nothing is more admirable in his character or more beloved in his history than the touching affection he revealed all his life for the unlettered pioneer woman who was his own mother. She died when he was still a child, but Lincoln seems to have had an almost Catholic sense of her presence by prayer in his later life. He is said to have paid to her memory the frequently quoted tribute: "All that I am, all that I hope to be, I owe to my angel mother."

Lincoln represents the type of the truly great in civic life. Among the priests and princes of the Church no one in modern times is more beloved than Pope Pius X. Sometimes in St. Peter's great church in Rome it seems as if all other shrines, save that of the Apostle himself, have been temporarily deserted in order that pilgrims may gather at the tomb of Pius X to pray for the beatification of this great Pope, so rich in God's grace, so beautiful in human qualities.

Pius X bore the proudest, most lofty title which mankind knows: Vicar of Christ on earth, Chief Shepherd of all Christendom. Yet on his desk in the apostolic palace from which he ruled the Church of God, the holy priest kept with affectionate piety a picture of his peasant mother wearing the humble shawl that characterizes all the mothers of the poor in the region where he was born.[3]

We need not multiply examples. Everyone will understand what we mean if only he examine his own heart. When the love of passion has spent its force and all love of utility has passed, when every due love of spouse or friend or other comrade is acknowledged, there still remains the unique love of the normal human heart for the mother who gave it flesh.

What must have been the love of the most perfect human heart, the love of Jesus Christ, for His Virgin Mother! The devotion of imperfect men to their mothers can only suggest the divine consideration which Christ, conceived by the Holy Spirit, born of the Virgin Mary, must have given her to whom He owed the flesh by which we were redeemed.

For those who understand the human heart, quite as much as for those who understand divine revelation, there will be no confusion about the dogma of the Assumption, the conviction of Catholics that Christ did not allow His holy one to undergo corruption. The definition by the Holy Father has only confirmed what the instinct of Christians had always suggested to them and what their constant tradition has actually taught them.

We reason with minds illumined by faith and thus we come to understand what Christ *could* do as God for her whom He specially loved, the sinless woman who gave Him His human flesh and blood. We know from sacred history and from devout reflection what Christ as man *would* do for His Blessed Mother, the first fruit of His

New Testament, the first redeemed by His atoning merits, the fairest of all His flock. And so we acknowledge that the God-Man *did* in fact accord to His Mother, early after her death, what we confidently believe will eventually be accorded to all others whom He has redeemed by His Precious Blood: the privilege of resurrection from the dead and bodily assumption into heaven.

By the Assumption of the Blessed Virgin the Church means, then, that Mary, the Mother of Christ, after she had died was restored to life by God's power and taken intact to heaven. She enjoyed the privilege of an *anticipated resurrection*, thus receiving by favor the glorious destiny which the Bible foretells for all the Just in the General Judgment at the end of the world.

In a word, this daughter of Eve died as all must, but having died, she was spared the corruption which is the fate of sinful flesh. This is the third victory in which Mary by privilege mirrors the victories of her Divine Son, the Sun of Justice. First is her total victory over sin; this the Church defined in the dogma of her Immaculate Conception. Then there is her complete victory over concupiscence; this the Church proclaims in the dogmas respecting her Perpetual Virginity. Implicit in these dogmatic truths is Mary's victory over death, achieved in her Assumption.

And so, after she had closed her eyes in the sleep of death, Christ's predilection for His Blessed Mother prompted the wonders in her behalf which we commemorate in the last two mysteries of the rosary.

All the Church rejoices in this confirmation and clarification of the Christian tradition concerning Mary, the Mother of God. That tradition had been well founded. The faithful have cherished the relics of the saints and martyrs from the first beginnings of the Church, but they have never pretended to possess any trace of the body of the Queen of all saints, the Mother of all martyrs. Everyone will appreciate the force of this impressive fact: Catholics have piously sought out and jealously guarded the remains of their lesser saints, from apostolic times to our own day. Had the body of Mary been anywhere on this earth the devout would have made a search for it as untiring as the quest of Saint Helena for the relics of the True Cross, nor would Catholics have rested until Mary's hallowed remains had been enshrined in a manner befitting her love for Jesus and our love for her.

Both Eastern and Western Christendom have eloquently proclaimed their faith in the Assumption of Mary and the compelling reasons for their convictions in its regard. Among the great Fathers of Eastern Christendom none is more renowned for mastery of the orthodox traditions of the Church than Saint John of Damascus. Preaching almost thirteen centuries ago on the Feast of the Assumption, Saint John cried out to Mary: "Thy sacred sleeping may not be called death, but migration to another country. . . . The death of the other saints is blessed because it brings them to blessedness, but death has not beatified thee; thou hast glorified death, dispelling its sadness and turning it to joy. . . . How could corruption dare to sully the body that carried Life itself?"[4]

Western Christendom has no witness to the ancient faith more conspicuous than Saint Augustine for fidelity to Scripture and Tradition. Augustine frequently preached on the Assumption of Mary, and he once explained it in these eloquent terms:

If the death of all the saints is precious, the death of Mary is beyond price. . . . Mary, by the bounty of Christ, was assumed into the joy of eternity and was received more honorably than others, since she was honored above all others by grace. . . . She was not dragged down to the common lot of humanity which is corruption, since she had borne her Savior and the Savior of all. If the will of God had chosen to preserve unscathed the vesture of the children in the fiery furnace, why should He deny to His own Mother what He had willed for the garments of strangers? By His sole mercy He willed to preserve Jonah incorrupt within the whale; and shall He not by grace preserve incorrupt Mary, His Mother?[5]

What should the definition of the Assumption mean to each of us? It serves as a solemn and consoling pledge of our own eventual resurrection from the dead and of the restoration to us of our loved ones, glorified in their own flesh, on the last day. It should quicken in each of us the age-old faith which fired the words of holy Job: "I know that my Redeemer liveth, and in the last day I shall rise out of the earth. And I shall be clothed again with my skin, and in my flesh I shall see my God."[6] It should enable us to repeat with new fervor and increased confidence the words of the Apostles' Creed: "I believe in . . . the resurrection of the body and in life everlasting."

The definition of Mary's anticipated resurrection is, then, a solemn reminder of the predestined reunion of our own bodies with the immortal souls which gave them life here below. It affirms the sanctity of the human body, its true dignity and eternal worth, at a moment in history when paganism has led to two superficially opposed extremes: a perverse cult of the body on the one hand, the cruel abuse of bodies on the other. This papal definition reminds us how highly God Himself values the human bodies He has fashioned to be temples of the Holy Spirit.

So, too, it offers further evidence of the Blessed Mother's benign influence in our lives. He Who is mighty has done great things for her; holy is His name.[7] We might be tempted to approach God with the fear and trembling of the pagans had it not been for the revelation of His infinite mercy in the Incarnation of Christ and of His tender affection in the privileges accorded Christ's Mother. Therefore the definition of the Assumption should prompt us the more confidently to seek Mary's prayers, to ask her heavenly aid with ever more childlike simplicity.

Queen of the Angels, we beg her affection for our children. *Mother Most Pure*, we ask her guidance for our young people. *House of Gold* and *Tower of Ivory*, may she bring strength to our homes. *Cause of Our Joy*, may she lift the weight of worry from human hearts. *Morning Star*, *Star of the Sea*, we seek her guidance for our leaders and for all who direct the destinies of mankind in these dark days. *Virgin Most Prudent*, our teachers need her patronage. *Help of the Sick*, we commend to her our doctors and nurses, as well as the patients committed to their care. *Spouse of the Carpenter of Nazareth*, she must especially love our working people. *Queen of Apostles*, may she console and inspire our priests. *Virgin Most Faithful*, she protects our nuns and all who live under religious vows. *Queen of Martyrs*, the persecuted Catholics of whole areas of the world turn to her for the grace of perseverance. *Queen of Peace*, *Mother of Mankind*, may her powerful intercession speed the day of international reconciliation and Christian world order. *Queen of Heaven*,

44

Our Lady of the Assumption, the thought of her should console all hearts that are homesick for heaven, hungry for union with God.[8]

Finally, the honors paid to Mary should greatly increase devotion to Jesus, her Adorable Son, Our Savior. All her privileges are because of Him. All her power comes from Him. All her graces, all her sanctity, flow from the grace of Christ. If her devout lovers send their prayers through Mary to Jesus, *ad Jesum per Mariam*, it is only because Jesus came to us through her. Christ remains the first and the final object of all Catholic cult, of our praise and our prayers. Never is this more true than when we adore Him by honoring His Mother.

Catholics have always remembered Mary with reverence whenever they have thought of Jesus with adoration; they never think of Mary with veneration but what they remember Jesus with worship. So it has always been: "They found the Child (Jesus) with Mary His Mother and falling down they adored Him."[9] Thus does the Sacred Scripture record the introduction of the Gentile world to Christ. "Now there stood by the Cross of Jesus, His Mother."[10] So the Bible describes the last moments of His life on earth. And ever since in Christian history these two names have been lovingly associated in the thought of the devout. *Jesus! Mary!*—these were the powerful names on the proud banner of Saint Joan of Arc. *Jesus with Mary be with us in our journey!*—This was the efficacious prayer with which Columbus set forth to open up our hemisphere; it was the constant inspiration of his epoch-making voyage.[11] *Jesus, Mary, and Joseph*— with these sweet names on their lips millions of our blessed dead have taken leave of life. So shall it always be, the more so because of this definition.

45

And so, as all the world acclaims the Blessed Mother, assumed into heaven to reign as Queen of the Angels, we speak our word of praise to her and prayer to Christ:

O Jesus, Son of God, Whose love for us made Thee share our humanity here on earth, give us the grace one day to share Thy divinity in heaven. Jesus, Son of Man, Whose tender love for Mary made Thee bring her bodily to heaven, give us back on the last day, holy and perfect, those whom we love that we may enjoy, together with them, the company of Thy Blessed Mother and all Thy saints before the throne of God.

O Holy Virgin, in the midst of thy glory, forget not the sorrows of the earth. Look down with gentle care on those who suffer, on those who live in the midst of difficulties and whose lips tremble with the fears of life. Have pity on those who love one another but are separated. Have pity on the loneliness of human hearts, on the weakness of our faith, on the objects of our affection. Have pity on those who weep, on those who pray, on those who hope. Give peace to the Church and victory to the truth; protect our homes against all sin, our land against all enemies; grant us the joy of seeing thee at last in heaven, forever and ever. *Amen!*

III

Mariology in the English-Speaking World

A convention of this kind might welcome a session given over entirely to the review of the praise of Our Blessed Lady by poetry. In such a session the English-speaking world would be proudly represented. Many of those who have inherited the poet's vocation of Chaucer have inherited together with it his desire to sing in our language the glory of our blissful Lady, Jesus' Mother dear.[1]

A certain humility and characteristic understatement have marked the poets of our language who sing of Mary, since first Chaucer confessed the temperamental limitation, if it be such, of our race:

> Lady! Thy goodness, thy magnificence, thy virtue,
> > and thy great humility,
> Surpass all science and all utterance. . . .
> > My knowledge is so weak, O blissful Queen!
> > To tell abroad thy mighty worthiness,
> > That I the weight of it may not sustain.[2]

Thus the poets of our language ever since: Lydgate, Constable, Rowlands, and, in their days, Gerard Manley Hopkins, G. K. Chesterton, and some of our devout contemporaries.

But poetry is not the direct interest of this convention. Neither, I take it, is the literature of devotion, though

This paper was delivered at Worcester, Massachusetts, on January 3, 1951, during the second convention of the Mariological Society of America.

47

in this fair field, too, those who pray to God and speak to His saints in the many accents of our language have told their love of God's Mother. Out of the not inconsiderable number of Marian devotional classics in English, each will probably remember the one or more to which he is personally indebted for warm light and loving understanding. And so where some would recall other writers, another thinks of Father Faber or of Father Henry Coleridge and his *The Mother of the King* and *The Mother of the Church*.

Nor, again, is our present interest in the evidences of practical devotion to Mary in the English-speaking world. Presumably Daniel Sargent's *Our Land and Our Lady* most succinctly records the American chapters in the history of devotion to Mary. That story in its English chapters needs no retelling to one who remembers Walsingham or the unusually rich history of English understanding of Our Lady's Assumption, from the days of King Alfred through those of Lanfranc and later Henry VI and Lupton's Tower at Eton.

But, alas, the English-speaking world has largely broken with the orthodox faith of Catholic Christendom. Heresy in doctrine and devotion concerning the Blessed Mother has had, however, occasional curious and seemingly contradictory characteristics. Together with an almost frigid repudiation of devotion to Mary, a refreshing desire to restore Mary to her proper place in the Christian faith sometimes reveals itself in heterodoxy. For instance, one remembers a book of meditation on the Blessed Mother, her virtues and her predestination, published in the last century by the Episcopal Bishop of Vermont, of all places. True, the case is exceptional, but it is by no means unique.

So, too, there are grounds for hope, one feels, in the confession by many seekers for the truth of a genuine *embarrassment* with regard to the Blessed Mother. Thus in 1930 a significant article, "Why I Would Find It Difficult to Become a Roman Catholic", by Dr. William E. Orchard, avowed difficulties concerning Catholic devotion to Mary; in point of fact the author was already well on the way to faith concerning Catholic *doctrine* on Mary.

Before him, John Henry Newman had confessed to like embarrassment. In his autobiography, Newman writes:

> At least during the Tract Movement, I thought the essence of her (the Roman Church's) offence to consist in the honors which she paid to the Blessed Virgin and the saints, and the more I grew in devotion, both to the saints and to Our Lady, the more impatient was I at the Roman practices, as if those glorified creations of God must be gravely shocked, if pain could be theirs, at the undue veneration of which they were the objects. Such devotional manifestations in honor of Our Lady had been my great *crux* as regards Catholicism.[3]

One mentions this point because, paradoxical though it sounds in the face of the sometimes rude and even violent repudiation by non-Catholics of the recent dogmatic definition of the Christian faith concerning the Assumption, one remains persuaded that the English-speaking world may yet return to its erstwhile convictions concerning *Christ* and to the sanctity and sanity of *Christendom* precisely through a greater appreciation of the moral and social corollaries of sound *Mariology*.

One ventures to cite John Henry Newman as the

example of how this might yet be. In our rereading of his *Parochial and Plain Sermons* the impression grows that Newman as an Anglican was probably the last Protestant theologian of stature to speak of Jesus, of Mary, and of God's grace as had ancient Christendom; just so he became probably the first Catholic in generations, please God not the last, to speak and write of these with the native verve, the disciplined restraint, the special genius and particular beauty of the language of the English-speaking world.[4] At least for these two reasons, Newman must always be a symbol of hope to those whose solicitude for the Church includes a particular zeal for the souls outside the Church who, though deprived of the ancient, the perennial faith, nonetheless share with us the language of Chaucer and Shakespeare, together with the racial characteristics, at least, of Venerable Bede and Thomas More.

To Catholic and non-Catholic alike, Newman appeals by reason of his profound convictions and his candid simplicity. His Christian character shines through every page of his works. More pertinent to our present considerations, we may take him without much debate as the prince of English-speaking theologians and, I venture to say, of our Mariologists in particular. Father Francis Friedel's notable dissertation on *The Mariology of Cardinal Newman* deserves fresh attention at this time, especially the section on the psychological evolution of Newman's Marian doctrine and devotion.[5] The spiritual case history of the great convert-Cardinal may yet prove more typical than it has to date, as God's graces are poured forth in proportion to the evils and vexations of the last half of the twentieth century.

In the Mariology of Cardinal Newman one encounters

first, last, and always a strictly Christological spirit and emphasis. As an Anglican he had argued, "The more [Mary] is considered in her person, the more dangerous is such knowledge for us; she is so close to God, too pure and holy a flower to be more than *seen* on earth. We hardly seem able to put her in her proper position. We cannot combine in our thought of her all we should ascribe with all we should withhold. Consequently, we are to think of her only with her Divine Son."[6]

But later, as he came to understand the heinous ravages and unhappy origins of heresy, Newman turned his devout inquiry more directly to Mary, only to discover how intimately Christocentric had been the development of Catholic Christendom's Mariology. He came to see that the exaltation of Mary had been dependent upon the glory of her Divine Son; only when it was necessary to secure a right faith in Jesus had the manifestation of her privileges and prerogatives taken place. Newman said:

When His name was dishonoured, then it was that she did Him service; when Emmanuel was denied, then the Mother of God (as it were) came forward; when heretics said that God was not incarnate, then was the time for her own honours. And then, when as much as this had been accomplished, she had done with strife; she fought not for herself. No fierce controversy, no persecuted confessors, no heresiarch, no anathema were necessary for her gradual manifestation . . . she has raised herself aloft silently and has grown into her place in the Church by a tranquil influence and a natural process. . . . Thus was she reared without hands, and gained a modest victory, and exerts a gentle sway, which she has not claimed. When a dispute arose about her among her children, she

51

hushed it; when objections were urged against her, she
waived her claims and waited.[7]

And so, Newman came to reunion with Rome partly,
at least, through understanding love for Mary. He came
to Mary, as to all the Catholic creed, through his desire
to see the firm basis of dogma concerning Christ restored
to the crumbling walls of Christendom. Dogma was the
fundamental interest of his mind. Of all the mysteries of
faith, his attention was most concentrated on the central
truth of the gospel—the Incarnation, which Newman
considered the article by which the Church stood or fell.

It was, then, from his clear understanding of Christology that Newman came to Mariology—and specifically
out of his luminous appreciation of Christ's total *divinity*
and total *humanity*.

Father Friedel summarizes effectively Newman's development:

> Since it was most fitting that the Word should become
> incarnate in order to effect man's redemption, He might
> have come into the world in divers manners. Though He
> did not wish to have an earthly father, yet He wished to
> come by the way of generation lest He should miss
> the participation of our nature. As at the creation the
> Almighty formed woman out of man, so now by a like
> mystery but in a reverse order the new Adam was to be
> fashioned from the woman. The Word set apart Mary as
> His mother, "to yield a created nature to Him Who was
> her Creator. Thus He came into the world, not in the
> clouds of heaven, but born into it, born of a woman; He,
> the Son of Mary, and she . . . the Mother of God. Thus
> He came, selecting and setting apart for Himself the
> elements of body and soul; then uniting them to Himself
> from their first origin of existence, pervading them,

hallowing them by His own divinity, spiritualizing them and filling them with light and purity, the while they continued to be human."[8] God chose a daughter of man to become the Mother of God.[9] He was taking upon Him her flesh and "humbling Himself to be called her offspring."[10] Thereby He conferred upon her the greatest honor ever put upon any individual of our fallen race, so that it is difficult to say which is the more wonderful to admire—the unspeakable grace bestowed upon Mary or the great condescension of the Word, Who though Son of God wished also to become the Son of Mary.[11]

Let Newman himself describe the awesome mystery of all this:

At first sight we might be tempted to say that it throws into confusion our primary ideas of the Creator and the creature, the Eternal and the temporal, the Self-subsisting and the dependent; and yet, on further consideration, we shall see that we cannot refuse the title (Mother of the Creator) to Mary without denying the divine Incarnation.[12]

But there is something more wonderful than that Mary should be called and should be indeed the Mother of God. It is that God, without ceasing to be God, should become man. Yet this is an elementary truth of revelation; prophets, evangelists, and Apostles all testify that the Eternal Word has decreed to come to earth and become a man like any of us, to take a human soul and body and to make them His own[13]

"Faith teaches that the Blessed Virgin Mary is truly the Mother of God, the *Theotokos*, *Deipara*."[14] The Council of Ephesus defined it in clear, unmistakable terms: "If anyone doth not confess that God is in all truth Emmanuel and that because of this the Holy Virgin is Mother of God . . . let him be anathema."[15] The Council of Chalcedon confirmed it.[16] Newman calls this sanctioning of the *Theotokos* "an addition greater, perhaps, than any before or since to the letter of the primitive faith."[17] Elsewhere he says of this word: "It carries with it no admixture of rhetoric, no taint of extravagant affection—it has nothing else but a well-weighed, grave, dogmatic sense, which corresponds and is adequate to its sound. It intends to express that God is Mary's Son, as truly as any of us is the son of his mother."[18]

And so the dogma of Mary as Mother of God follows from the Christian dogma concerning Christ. This is always one of its functions: The Catholic dogma concerning Mary keeps the dogma concerning Christ from degenerating into the amorphous state of heretical Christology. Mariology prevents a dreamy, unreal way of regarding the whole mystery of the Incarnation. It protects the doctrine *De Verbo Incarnato* and keeps the faith of Catholics from specious humanitarianism or vague theological abstractions.

Enamored of the Fathers of the Church, of their science and speculation, Newman had the patristic sense of the basic dogmas concerning the *humanity* and the *divinity* of Jesus and perceived how Mariology is bound up with them. He declares:

The confession that Mary is *Deipara*, or the Mother of God, is that safeguard wherewith we seal up and secure the doctrine of the Apostle from all evasion and that test whereby we detect all the pretense of those bad spirits of "Anti-Christ which have gone out into the world." It declares that He is God; it implies that He is man; it suggests that He is God still, though He has become man, and that He is true man though He is God. . . . . If Mary is the Mother of God, Christ must be literally Emmanuel, God with us.[19]

The most effectual means the Church had of expelling false teachers concerning Christ's nature was by using the word *Theotokos* against them. Newman expresses this aptly when he says: "The Church and Satan agreed together on this, that Son and Mother went together; and the experience of three centuries has confirmed their testimony, for Catholics who have honoured the Mother still worship the Son, while Protestants who now have ceased to confess the Son began by scoffing at the Mother."[20]

Mary's special office in the Church is still to protect the doctrine concerning her Divine Son; so Newman would have us understand. She reminds us ever that there was One Who, on becoming her Son, "did not abhor the Virgin's womb."[21] She is the *Turris Davidica*, the high and strong defense of the King of Israel. With good reason, then, can the Church say of her that she destroys all heresies in the whole world.[22]

This conception of Mary's special function is not, of course, peculiar to Newman. St. John Damascene had already suggested the idea when he wrote: "It is with good reason that we give St. Mary the name of Mother of God, for this title suffices to establish in all its integrity the mystery of the Word made flesh."[23]

The elements of Newman's theory of Mary's place in the work of the redemption are again strictly Christ-ocentric and follow closely on Sacred Scripture. His doctrine on the co-redemptive role of Mary is stated in terms of Mary as the second Eve and is based on a tightly reasoned parallelism between the circumstances of the Fall and those of the redemption as they are set forth in Sacred Scripture and are elaborated by his beloved Church Fathers.

Adam as head of the human race had been, of course, primarily responsible for the fate of posterity; he was our representative. By his fall, the race forfeited the privileges conferred originally upon us by God; had he not fallen, though Eve might have yielded to the tempter's wiles, grace would not have been lost to humanity. Eve was not head of the race as Adam was; still, she had her cooperative position in the First Covenant. Adam named her the "mother of all the living"[24] to show not only her relation to the human race but also her dignity. She had her special place as regards its trial and fall in Adam; she had an integral share in the primeval events. She listened to the serpent, ate of the forbidden fruit, and offered it to her husband. Newman argues:

> She cooperated, not as an irresponsible instrument, but intimately and personally in the sin: she brought it about. As the history stands, she was a *sine qua non*, a positive, active cause of it. And she had her share in the punishment; in the sentence pronounced on her, she was recognized as a real agent in the temptation and its issue, and she suffered accordingly.[25]

Three actors are represented in this tragic scene of the proto-evangelium, a scene fraught with so many consequences for the billions of human beings that would people the globe in future ages. There was the serpent, the woman, and the man. When the sentence was pronounced on each of these three individually, an event was announced for some distant future when the three same parties would meet again—the serpent, the woman, and the man; but it was to be a second Adam and a second Eve, and the new Eve was to be the mother of the new Adam, for the Lord had said: "I will put enmity between thee and the woman and between thy seed and her seed."[26]

As Adam primarily brought about the Fall, so the new Adam would be the principal and absolutely essential cause of redemption. However, Eve had her share in the first sin; in like manner, the new Eve was to have her place in the economy of redemption. Eve was responsible and instrumental in Adam's sin; the new Eve, too, was to be a voluntary agent; she was to be united with her Divine Son in spirit and in will, as she was associated with Him in body, by furnishing Him the elements of His human nature.[27] "As Eve opened the way for the fatal deed of the first Adam, so it was fitting that Mary should open the way for the great achievement of the second Adam, even Our Lord Jesus Christ."[28] So Newman presents the matter.

For him Mary is the second and better Eve, taking the initial part in the world's restoration. God ever demands a reasonable service and the voluntary cooperation of creatures in His works; He forces no will but requires acquiescence in His designs. Though the Incarnation was to be of such tremendous significance for the whole human race, nevertheless as for man's fall, so for the restoration, He allowed the accomplishment or nonaccomplishment of His will to rest solely on the *Fiat* of a young maiden. When God sent the angel to announce the great dignity that was to be Mary's portion, He wished that she should enter upon her function as mother to the Redeemer knowingly and willingly. Mary pondered the full import of the angel's message and, with the consent of a heart full of God's love, she answered: "Behold the handmaid of the Lord; be it done to me according to thy word."[29]

It is at once evident from the mere Gospel narrative that Mary was not only the physical instrument of the Word's taking flesh but also an instrumental, responsible cause. This Newman considered to be the view of the Fathers. Protestants lose sight of this important fact. Newman was obliged to call Pusey to task for his assertion in the *Eirenicon* that "the Fathers speak of the Blessed Virgin as the instrument of our salvation in that she gave birth to the Redeemer and apply personally to her the title of Chosen Vessel of the Incarnation."[30] Newman, even as an Anglican, had not shared this view of his friend, though he speaks of her as an instrument, as is every saint, working toward an end appointed by God. But he did not consider her exclusively as such; he had already remarked the parallelism between Eve and Mary: "Jesus is the seed of the woman announced to guilty Eve . . . in [Mary] the destinies of the world were to be reversed and the serpent's head bruised . . . in her the curse pronounced on Eve was changed to a blessing . . . in bearing Our Lord, she has taken off or lightened the peculiar disgrace which the woman inherited for seducing Adam, in that she was ruled over by man."[31]

Newman turned to the Fathers for his understanding that Mary was more than a mere physical instrument. "They declare", says he,

> that she was not a mere instrument in the Incarnation, such as David or Judah may be considered; . . . she

58

cooperated in our salvation not merely by the descent of the Holy Ghost upon her body but by specific holy acts, the effect of the Holy Ghost within her soul; that, as Eve forfeited privileges by sin, so Mary earned privileges by the fruits of grace; that, as Eve was disobedient and unbelieving, so Mary was obedient and believing; that, as Eve was a cause of ruin to all, Mary was a cause of salvation to all; that, as Eve made room for Adam's fall, so Mary made room for Our Lord's reparation of it; and thus, whereas the free gift was not as the offence, but much greater, it follows that, as Eve cooperated in effecting a great evil, Mary cooperated in effecting a much greater good.[32]

From her cooperation with the Redeemer, Catholics have come to style Mary *co-Redemptress*, a title to which Pusey protested in his *Eirenicon*. Newman could not see why there should be any objection to calling her *co-Redemptress* when the Fathers of the Church had called her by such names as *Mother of God*, *Second Eve*, *Mother of Life*, *the Morning Star*, *the Mystical New Heaven*, *the Scepter of Orthodoxy*.

For Newman, Mary does not usurp the place of her Divine Son in the work of redemption. She is not the cause of grace. Jesus alone is the life of the soul; He alone regenerates us; Mary is our mother by divine appointment, and her office is external to us. This is elementary dogma known by the simplest Catholic. No matter how high we elevate Mary—and we may raise her to a height just short of the infinite—she remains ever a creature as one of us, though a very privileged one.

Her function of mediatrix or co-redemptress was not absolutely necessary, *necessitate medii*, as the schoolmen would say; yet it was really necessary according to the designs of Divine Providence. The Fathers manifest this clearly when they speak of her as the cause of salvation to the human race. From the doctrine of the second Eve springs that of the spiritual maternity. She is truly the Mother of men; like Eve, she has become the Mother of all the living. By becoming the Mother of God and therefore instrument of the Incarnation, she has entered into an intimate relationship with *us*, each and all, in what concerns our spiritual life, for through the Incarnation we become brethren of Christ and heirs of heaven.

Mother of the physical Christ, she is not less Mother of the Mystical Christ. It is suggested, in all deference, that a future gathering of this group might well explore the rich theological implications of Mary's spiritual maternity.

Cardinal Newman will provide many and rewarding leads in such exploration. Theological literature offers few pages so ingenious or so attractive as those which preserve Newman's reflections on Mary and the Church.

Newman saw the relation between Mary and the Church, as others before him, such as St. Caesarius of Arles, who speaks of these "two mothers".[33] St. Augustine has given us in a masterly page the doctrine on the relation between Mary and the Church:

> The Church imitates the Mother of Christ, her Spouse and Lord. The Church also is both mother and virgin. Of whose purity do we take such jealous care if she is not a virgin? and to whose children do we speak if she is not a mother? Mary has given corporal birth to the head of this body; the Church brings forth spiritually the members of this head. For both, virginity is no hindrance to fruitfulness; for both, fruitfulness does not tarnish their virginity. . . . But to one woman alone, to Mary, belongs

the right to be both spiritually and corporally, mother and virgin. Spiritually, she is not mother of our head, of Our Savior, from whom she was rather spiritually born, but she is certainly mother of His members, that is, she is our mother; for she has cooperated by her love in giving birth to the faithful in the Church. . . . Mary is, then, in body and soul, mother and virgin, Mother of Christ and Virgin of Christ. As for the Church, in the person of the saints who will possess the kingdom of God, she is in spirit Mother of Christ (i.e., by doing the will of God according to the expression in St. Matthew) and wholly Virgin of Christ.[34]

By consenting to the Incarnation and becoming the Mother of God, Mary becomes mother of men, since she willed the regeneration of men; the Church is on earth to continue the work in which Mary had cooperated. The superiority, however, lies on the side of Mary. She is united to the Conqueror and triumphs with Him; the Church succeeds in continuing to struggle. Mary has her place in the work of redemption, in the acquisition and distribution of grace; the Church participates only in the distribution. In the acquisition and distribution of grace Mary is associated, though only in a secondary manner, to Jesus Christ, principal cause and source of all merit; in the distribution of grace the Church is but an instrument. Mary is mother of the Savior and of the members of His Mystical Body; the Church is mother of the members only.

This is what is meant by Newman when he maintains that the Apostle would not have spoken of the Church under this particular image unless there had existed a Blessed Virgin Mary. Under the symbol of the Woman, the real sense applies to the Church. But Mary is not an inferior personage taken as symbol of something greater; she is rather taken as the model of all who are to follow her; as a sovereign, she unites in herself all the forces and the will of the whole Church. The thought of the Church and of Mary complete and recall each other. Such is the meaning of the Fathers and theologians as well as of the Church's liturgy when applying this chapter of the Apocalypse to the Blessed Virgin. Hence, Newman can say that the Woman and Child are more than mere personifications; they are *real persons*. Thus, it is not a mere accommodation of the text to the Blessed Virgin; when St. John contemplated in the heavens of the Woman clothed with the sun, he found in her a resemblance to the one whom he could call his own mother.

It is not easy to forego the pleasure of following Newman into the pages of his *Discourses to Mixed Congregations* and the *Meditations and Devotions* in order to enjoy the sheer beauty of his treatment of the personal relations between Jesus and Mary, the qualities of Mary's sanctity, and the circumstances of her death. Perhaps passing reference may be made in our present moment of Marian history to Newman's consideration on the Assumption, a dogma he was quick to see as crowning and following from all the privileges of Mary, beginning with the Immaculate Conception.

The comparison between Mary and Eve once more recurs to Newman in this connection. Adam and Eve both had been created upright and sinless; had they been faithful to God's command, they would have been immortal in spite of the corruptibility of their bodies. Only when they had sinned did their bodies follow the

ordinary law of their corruptible nature. From thenceforth all who share in their curse must share in the
punishment.

> If Eve, the beautiful daughter of God, never would have
> become dust and ashes unless she had sinned, shall we not
> say that Mary, having never sinned, retained the gift
> which Eve, by sinning, lost? What had Mary done to
> forfeit the privilege given to our first parents in the
> beginning? Was her comeliness to be turned into cor-
> ruption and her fine gold to become dim without reason
> assigned? Impossible. Therefore, we believe that, though
> she died for a short hour as did Our Lord Himself, yet
> like Him and by His almighty power she was raised again
> from the grave.[35]

Extrinsic arguments from history weigh heavily with
Newman, and his reasoning from these concerning the
Assumption is typical:

> If her body was not taken into heaven, where is it? how
> comes it that it is hidden from us? why do we not hear of
> her tomb as being here or there? why are not pilgrimages
> made to it? why are not relics producible of her, as of the
> saints in general? Is it not even a natural instinct which
> makes us reverent toward the places where our dead are
> buried?

Our Lord's tomb was honored; in like manner the tombs
and relics of John the Baptist, the Apostles, and martyrs.

> Now if there was any one who more than all would be
> preciously taken care of, it would be Our Lady. Why,
> then, do we hear nothing of the Blessed Virgin's body
> and its separate relics? Is it conceivable that they who had
> been so reverent and careful of the bodies of the saints and

the martyrs should neglect her—her who was Queen of the Martyrs and Queen of the Saints, who was the very Mother of Our Lord? It is impossible. Why, then, is she thus the *hidden Rose*? Plainly because that sacred body is in heaven, not on earth.[36]

The Assumption does not, of course, terminate the relation of Mary to the Church. On the contrary, it gives this relation a new meaning, a more intimate character. Newman sums up briefly but beautifully the interrelations of the communion of saints, the prayer of Christians, and the privileges of Mary:

> I consider it impossible, then, for those who believe the Church to be one vast body in heaven and on earth, in which every holy creature of God has his place and of which prayer is the life, when once they recognize the sanctity and dignity of the Blessed Virgin, not to perceive immediately that her office is one of perpetual intercession for the faithful militant and that our very relation to her must be that of clients to a patron, and that, in the eternal enmity which exists between the woman and the serpent, while the serpent's strength lies in being the tempter, the weapon of the second Eve and Mother of God is prayer.[37]

At least in the possession of this weapon in common with Mary, we have a ground for hope whatever evils close about us. May we who speak the language of Newman speak it in prayer—particularly in prayer to Mary and through her to Jesus, her Son, Our Brother.

IV

Lourdes, Land of the Rosary

Behind the branches, in the opening, I saw a white girl, not bigger than I, who made me a little bow with her head. . . . A rosary was hanging on her right arm. . . . I put my hand in my pocket and took out the rosary that I always carry in it. . . . I said my rosary. The girl made the beads of hers slip through her fingers, but she did not move her lips. While saying my rosary I was looking as hard as I could.

Thus Bernadette described the first of the historic apparitions which have so directed, one might almost say dominated, the character and quality of contemporary devotion to Mary. From that simple scene have increasingly come devotions which have brought the rosary into the homes, streets, factories, and public places of remote hamlets and mighty cities in every corner of the modern world. Block rosaries in Detroit and in New England towns; the rosary recited by groups of sailors on American battleships; the rosary that is the pause that truly renews workers in a French factory of which I read not long ago; the rosary repeated in the cars of a train carrying Irish, English, and Scottish pilgrims to Lourdes; the rosary that gave one soul to the bodies of several score Italian sick in the Lourdes asylum which I visited two years ago; the rosary led on the radio by Hollywood stars at Christmastime; the rosary said in the privacy of so many Christian homes in the confidence

This address was delivered at Worcester, Massachusetts, on April 8, 1951, before the Iraqi Club.

that *the family that prays together stays together*—all these are in direct line of descent from that rosary which Bernadette said, alone and afraid, at the dawn of the modern Age of Mary in a then wild, neglected corner of a town in the Pyrenees.

One thinks of all these things, tender, touching, and true, as he walks about the sacred *domaine de la grotte* during a pilgrimage to Lourdes. Rome is assuredly the city of Christ, the head of the Church, whose vicar dwells there and whose truth is there defined and defended. As in 1854, so now and always, we look to Rome to learn whatever Christ has revealed concerning Himself, His Church, His Mother, or ourselves. But, in the present Age of Mary at least, there is no denying the preeminent degree to which Lourdes, the land of the rosary, has become the heart of the praying Catholic world. Mary, the Mother of Christ and of all the redeemed, is unmistakably there; and there in 1958, as in 1858, one finds love confirming at the Grotto of Lourdes what truth defines at Rome.

Every Catholic understands the sense in which these things are true. The presence of Christ at Rome in special and surpassing fashion does not exclude the presence of Mary, His Mother. She is necessarily present wherever He is present to whom she gave flesh and blood as well as, humanly speaking, the breath of life itself. The love of her is also present wherever He rules, Himself or through His vicar. She is present, acknowledged, and loved in the Roman catacombs. She is paid homage in Roman basilicas, supremely, of course, in the regal temple which is *Major* of all the churches which bear the name of Saint Mary. She is remembered at almost every Roman corner where the *madonnelle* of the street shrines bring the Queen of Heaven so close to the life of Rome's very alleyways. She is lifted in triumphant glory atop her column in the Spanish Square, and Michelangelo gave her an exquisite corner and the best of his genius in the Pietà, which adds a touch of humane simplicity to the staggering majesty of Saint Peter's. But Rome is the city of Peter and therefore of Christ, Peter's Lord, Master, and Principal. There is never the slightest doubt about the claims of Peter or the authority of Christ at any point in Rome to which the pilgrim turns.

Lourdes, land of the rosary, is the city of Mary. Again, her priority of presence at Lourdes excludes neither Christ nor, for that matter, Peter. Christ is necessarily present wherever she is loved to whom He gave meaning and vocation, together with every privilege and power which is hers. Christ is present at Lourdes in the stations of the cross, the dramatic markings of the stages of His Passion, in following which the Lourdes pilgrim climbs even higher than the grotto of the shrine. He is present, glorious and full of mercy, in the Blessed Sacrament, enshrined in the Rosary Basilica or carried among the sick on the terrace of tears and hopes where His name is so passionately invoked in the traditional Lourdes prayers. Christ is certainly present authoritatively in the prelates and priests who officiate in the shrine ceremonies; He is present mystically in the masses of the poor, the sick, the halt, lame, and blind who crowd about the sacred springs.

Peter is present at Lourdes, too. It was to attest to a truth defined by him, speaking through his successors, that the Rosary Basilica has been enriched with indulgences and given its unique place in the prayer life of the worldwide Church that he still rules. The prayer for him and for his Apostolic See is always on the lips of the pilgrim at Lourdes.

But Lourdes is the city of Mary, all the same. In lonely beauty her figure gives warmth and light to the somber cave of the grotto. The gentle bow by which she greeted Bernadette still comforts and encourages the least of us as we lift our eyes toward the mosaic above the high altar of the crypt. It was at her bidding that the beads were first said here and that all the building began. It is her invitation which still brings the millions to the banks of the Gave, and it is her personalized communication, so to say, of the grace and the mercy of God which sends away so many bodies made more strong and so many souls made more clean. It is her praises which are echoed in the haunting Lourdes hymn and her name which lingers longest on the pilgrim's lips.

But it is the rosary which makes Lourdes at all times the city of Mary. One instinctively draws his beads from his pocket as he enters the area of the shrine. He remembers that Bernadette acted in like spontaneous obedience to the sweet compulsion of Mary's presence in the place. "Then I thought of saying my prayers: I put my hand in my pocket and took out the rosary that I always carry in it".

And thus the pilgrim to Lourdes finds himself one with Bernadette across a hundred years—Bernadette whose language he cannot speak and who never heard, I suppose, of his land but whose hands are entwined by the beads which circle his and which link both, with those of all praying Christians, to the hands by which Mary implores of her Son the mercy and pardon all men crave.

The sense of this identity with one another of all those who love Mary and seek her Son's pardon becomes even more strong as one takes his minute place in the Rosary Procession at night, fusing the flame of his small taper with the river of light that winds around the approaches to the Rosary Basilica. So many things which devout reason accepts but only dimly understands become luminously clear in the light of the sea of candles which envelops the multitudes made one by the recitation of the rosary at Lourdes. Now one begins to grasp the communion of souls in prayer out of which the communion of saints arises: the solidarity in grace and glory to which we are called out of humanity's solidarity in sin and pain, the way in which one must lose himself in order to find himself, as Jesus taught. The flame of my penny candle is lost in the river of fire at the Lourdes Rosary Procession, yet thus acquires its meaning and illumines for me so many mysteries, so many sorrows.

Lourdes is the city of Mary and the land of her rosary. Through the rosary, it somehow recaptures what must have been the blessed atmosphere of those like towns and villages of the Holy Land through which Jesus and Mary passed. The place of the Annunciation; the hills of the Visitation; the grotto of the Nativity; the scenes of the betrayal, condemnation, and death of her Son; and finally the places of His triumphs and hers, the garden of the Resurrection, the tomb where she lay in brief death, heaven itself—all are close by us as we hear the joyful, sorrowful, and glorious mysteries of the rosary recited at Lourdes in more languages than the Apostles heard at Pentecost, but in that same spirit of faith and love which united them to Mary and Mary to them in the Cenacle two thousand years ago.

The rosary, recalling many New Testament chapters and memories, intensifies the New Testament mood that hovers all about the city of Mary. The emphasis of the New Testament is on mercy, forgiveness, and healing; these are the elements blended in the spirit abroad at Lourdes. The very petitions which the sick repeat in soul-stabbing accents, led by their priests at the afternoon devotions, are phrases from the New Testament. "Lord, that I may see!" "Lord, that I may hear!" "Lord, that I may walk!" "Hosanna! Hosanna to the Son of David!" Here we feel we are back in the land where the Son of Mary went about healing and helping all with whom He came in contact.

Here, too, the rosary and Lourdes reveal the deep identity of point and spirit with the New Testament which they have in common. The healing of affliction, the forgiveness of sin, the gospel given to the poor, the acceptable year of the Lord, the nearness of heaven to earth, and the easy access of prayerful humanity to powerful divinity—all these overflow the pages of the New Testament, and all are present along the paths that lead to the shrine at the heart of Lourdes. These are the promises of Scripture; they are the petitions of the rosary. These are the heartwarming realities which the pilgrim finds at Lourdes, this New Testament town which is the land of the rosary.

But all these things are also present in every part of the Church. The majestic *authority* of Christ, typified by Rome, and the gentle *compassion* of Christ, symbolized by Lourdes, are blended in the work of every diocese and of every parish; they mingle in every devout home. Here is perhaps the greatest of the lessons of Lourdes: The faith makes rigorous, difficult demands; it has been filled with "hard sayings" since first Christ expounded its authoritative teachings. But it is charged with great

70

mercies, and its graces include great peace and all the consoling hope of which Lourdes is but one more reminder.

V

Mary Immaculate
Patroness of the United States

The liturgy of the Church, as well as popular devotion, perpetuates the venerable tradition by which special patrons are invoked as special intercessors with God and celestial advocates, so to speak, for particular localities, groups, or works within that universal Church for which Christ Himself makes constant intercession before the throne of the Father.

Such patrons probably began to be chosen as an outgrowth from the early Church custom of honoring certain martyrs as the *titulars* of churches and places. During the first three centuries the faithful assembled for worship in private homes, in the places where their beloved dead were buried, or in other secluded areas where neither the persecution nor the contamination of paganism about them could invade the peace and quiet of Christian devotion. As occasion permitted, buildings were erected or adapted for Christian cult. These buildings were not dedicated to saints originally, as churches and institutions now are, but were set apart and cherished as *houses of God* or *houses of prayer*. Their Greek and Latin names indicate this primary dedication to them: *kyriaca*, *dominica*, *oratoria*.

It was only after Constantine accorded to Christians peaceful freedom in the practice of their religion and in

This article was written for and published in the October 1954 issue of the *Thomist*.

the construction of churches that these began to be dedicated to saints. The origin of the custom of so dedicating the gathering places of the faithful seems natural enough. The sites chosen for the construction of churches were usually places already beloved by the Christian community because of their association with the martyrs, greatest of the heroes among the Christians. The association might have been because they were the scenes of the triumphs of martyrs, of their glorious deaths, or because they were made holy in some other way by the lives and the memories of those who bore ultimate and most valiant witness to their faith by the testimony of martyrdom.

And so it came to pass that early in the history of the Church in Rome and elsewhere the buildings erected for Christian worship took their titles from titulars among the martyrs or other saints whose pious memories were associated with the places on which the churches were built or with the communities by whom these buildings were erected, supported, or frequented. It was inevitable, both as a matter of logic and as a matter of piety, that those who gave their names to churches and to institutions as their titulars should eventually be thought of as the special protectors and patrons of the places and peoples dedicated to them.

In general terms it may be said that down to the seventeenth century it was largely popular devotion, though under the guidance of ecclesiastical authority, which chose celestial patrons from among the holy men and women renowned in life for their miracles and for their special ties of piety to the communities or institutions of which they became the protectors. In

73

1638, however, Pope Urban VIII set down certain rules by which the faithful of the Church should be guided in the selections henceforth of patrons for churches, cities, or even countries. Pope Urban was careful in thus codifying future procedure to leave unchanged the long-established customs by which traditional patrons were already venerated so long as these customs were consistent with sound piety and theological principles.

The norms promulgated by Pope Urban systematized and clarified many of the considerations by which particular patrons had been chosen popularly in previous generations. Often a saint was chosen as the patron of a region or of a community because his body or one of his major relics was in the possession of those who chose him as their patron. Frequently, a saint was chosen as patron of a place where he had preached the gospel or had performed the labors of his dedicated life or had died in the odor of sanctity. Sometimes the selection of patrons reflects the popular devotions preached at the time when the choice was made.

The underlying doctrine sustaining and inspiring the custom of choosing celestial patrons is, of course, the dogma of the Communion of Saints. This dogma proclaims the spiritual bond which exists among all those who love God and are thus united to Him, whether by vision in heaven or by faith on earth and in purgatory. The solidarity which unites those who love God, whether they be in the Church Militant here below or in the Church Suffering and the Church Triumphant in purgatory and in heaven hereafter, causes one and all to be interested in the fate of each. Those who are still on earth, and therefore still able to merit by their prayers and their sacrifices, are the advocates of the holy souls detained in the prison of love that is purgatory. Those who now stand unspotted before God's merciful face serve as advocates for their brethren both in purgatory and on earth. Even their heavenly advocacy or patronage, a Christian instinct assures us, will inevitably be colored and intensified as a result of the ties between them and the places or persons on earth that perpetuate their names as titulars and patrons.

Against the background of this summary history and even more sketchily summarized doctrine it is interesting to recall how the Blessed Mother, under her title of the Immaculate Conception, came to be chosen as the celestial patroness of the United States. A preliminary observation is important and interesting. On November 8, 1760, Our Lady, under her same title of the Immaculate Conception, had been proclaimed principal patroness of all possessions of the Spanish Crown, including those in the Americas.

At the sixth provincial council of Baltimore, May 10, 1846 (with twenty-three bishops and the representatives of four religious orders present), the Blessed Virgin Mary, *conceived without original sin*, was chosen as the patroness of the province. On February 7, 1847, this selection of the Blessed Virgin Mary, under the title of her Immaculate Conception, was extended so as to make her a principal patroness of the whole United States of America. The first Plenary Council of Baltimore, May 9–20, 1852, confirmed all the enactments of the seven provincial councils.[1]

This choice of Our Lady, under the title of the Immaculate Conception, to be patroness of the United States is considered thus meditatively by Daniel Sargent in his book, *Our Land and Our Lady*:

In 1846, not long after the native American riots, there met in Baltimore the sixth provincial council. While it was meeting, the armies of the United States were entering New Mexico and California. We were taking over more lands which the Spaniards had dedicated to the Immaculate Conception. Those in the council were not thinking of the invading armies. They had no way of knowing even whether they were conquering or being conquered. Yet they seemed unconsciously in one act of theirs to be preparing our land to take over Spain's old responsibilities. Twenty years of the Deluge had tightened the bond between the Church in our country and the Mother of God. It was a spontaneous act, therefore, when in this council permission was sought from Rome that we be allowed to elect as our patroness, her, who to the immigrants was not only their life, their sweetness, and their hope but also their only true equality, only true liberty, only true fraternity, the "Blessed Virgin Conceived Without Sin".[2]

The fact that this petition for the designation of the Immaculate Conception as the patroness of the United States was made eight years before the solemn definition of the dogma in her regard has always been a further joy to Catholic Americans. One cannot doubt that it has also been a source of special graces to the United States and, one ventures to say, to the hierarchy which officially took the action by which this happy choice was made in 1846. It is surely not too much to suggest that the Blessed Mother must have exercised a providential patronage over the proceedings of the Plenary Council itself and, as a result, over the myriad aspects of Catholic American life subsequently influenced by it.

The theological premises of the invocation of patrons

which we have recalled remind us of the inward spiritual union of the faithful, as members of Christ's Mystical Body, with all other members of this body, including the elect and the confirmed in justice whose participation in the kingdom of God is absolutely certain and through whose intercession help may be given to the faithful still wayfaring on earth.

The intercessory power of the servants of Christ who have triumphed through His grace is great before the throne of God. How much greater is the power of her who is not only a servant of God but the mother of His incarnate Son? Christ gave His Mother to all Christians on Calvary. The universal Catholic people have taken Mary to themselves by their creed and their cult, but Catholic Americans have made her their especial patroness by the deliberate and formal action of the special representatives of her Son in His Church in the United States.

The ties that bind us to the Immaculate Mother are therefore many and strong. The needs of the Church and of the members of Christ's Mystical Body in the United States are many and urgent. There is no one who can intercede for us with Christ more effectively than His Mother. The consequences of her patronage for us cannot be exaggerated and should not be minimized. Catholic Americans are Mary's devotees by the added title of her election as our principal patroness.

What the spiritual princes of an older day and world, supported by the piety of the subjects of their kings, did for Mary in France and Spain, the bishops of America, seconded by the believing citizens of our democracy, have in our days done for her here. Sound reason and

77

simple faith agree in suggesting that Mary, as patroness of our land, will benignly insure among us victories for faith and freedom comparable to those which once she accomplished there.

VI

Mary and Modern Times

Modern times have been described as the Age of Mary. What does this phrase mean?

I suppose that it means, first of all, that the age in which we live is an age in which we Christians have grown in our understanding of the place of Mary in the life of the Church, in the work of the redemption, and in the divine scheme of things. It is now one hundred years since Pope Pius IX began the modern development of our understanding concerning the Blessed Mother by defining the dogma of her Immaculate Conception. It is but four years since our Holy Father Pope Pius XII defined the dogma of her Assumption into heaven. In between these two polar points of doctrine concerning Mary, a whole world of new understanding of the truth with respect to her and of new appreciation of her privileges has come into being.

Accordingly, we refer to modern times as the Age of Mary because it is in modern times that our Holy Mother the Church has brought us to a more mature understanding of her doctrine concerning the Blessed Mother of Christ.

Then, too, the Age of Mary is properly attributed to our times because of the mighty growth of devotion to the Blessed Mother of Christ in the modern world, a growth in loving piety of which the symbols and the

This article was written for and published in the 1955 issue of the *Annals of St. Anthony's Shrine*.

centers have been many, with three most notable. First of all Lourdes with the enormous impetus given by the Lourdes apparitions to modern devotion to the rosary. And then we have La Salette with its message of penance and the new direction which it gave to a modern appreciation of the necessity for penance. And finally, almost in our own day, Fatima with its warnings of war and yet its unmistakable hope, if not promise, of peace. Out of each of these, Lourdes, La Salette, and Fatima, there have grown, and around these there have flourished, the many devotions which have made modern times especially the Age of Mary.

We have already mentioned the recent increased devotion to the rosary. We might also recall the devotions of the miraculous medal and the scapular. We call to mind the devotion to Our Lady of Perpetual Help and the growing devotion of the First Saturdays in honor of Our Lady of Fatima as further proof of the enormous development in popular piety and worldwide devotion to the Blessed Mother in modern times, all justifying our speaking of the age in which we live as the Age of Mary.

But above all, I think, ours is the Age of Mary because the worries of our generation are such as invite her sweet mercies and such as call for the healing influence of the truths which the Holy Catholic Church preaches concerning the Mother of Christ. It is always dangerous to speak of the evils of the hour as if they were something entirely new and hitherto unheard of. They are not. The things which discourage us, the things which sicken us, are all of them as old as sin, as old as treason, as old as death, as old as defeat, as old as sickness, as old as war. These are, of course, the very things which worry us. These are the evils of the hour, and they are the oldest worries in the world.

They are the evils which from time immemorial the spirits of truth and virtue have associated with the three-fold source of all sin and all grief. The worries of our modern age are as old as the world; they are as old as the flesh; they are as old as the devil. We pay the evils of the world too great tribute when we pretend that they are new and strong and fresh. They are not! They are merely new manifestations, at the most new forms, of these old unholy three—the world, the flesh, and the devil. They take new emphases. They appear in changing and sometimes novel forms, but it is to these three, the world, the flesh, and the devil, in the modern guises of their old temptations, that the doctrine of Holy Mother Church concerning the Blessed Mother of Christ brings timely and powerful counteraction.

First consider the world: The worries of our generation which spring from the center and move about into the spirit of the world are worries due to the aggressive and fratricidal divisions which plague mankind. We have inherited all the old vertical divisions of the human race: the divisions of race, nations, languages, and empires. All these old vertical divisions which pit man against man and brother against brother, these are with us still because of the spirit of the world. To these vertical divisions, as if to complicate them, there have been added new horizontal divisions which now cut across nations, language groups, and empires to set class against class within the same nation, child against parent within the same family, generation against generation within the same community, liberal versus conservative within the same party.

And so, in an age which finds the world plagued by horizontal and vertical divisions which pit us against one another, the Church offers us the image of Mary, Queen of Time and Eternity, Lily of Israel, Rose of Sharon, Spouse of the Worker, a carpenter in Nazareth, and yet Mother of Mankind, hope of eventual reconciliation among the warring tribes, princess of all the redeemed.

One of the reasons why we welcome the greater emphasis on the queenship of Mary is that such emphasis on the universal queenship of the Blessed Mother will dramatically demonstrate how she is lifted out of and above national, racial, or partisan divisions. The Irish will still love her as Our Lady of Knock, but they will remember that before and above all titles she is the Universal Queen of all Mankind. The French will remember her as Our Lady of Chartres, but they will remember that even more fundamentally, so to speak, she is the Queen of all Mankind. The Russians will still think of Our Lady of Kazan with nostalgic piety, but they will come to understand that she is supremely the Queen of all Mankind. The Spaniards will still be proud of Our Lady of Montserrat, but they will not be permitted to forget that she is the Queen of all Mankind. The English will cherish their memories of Our Lady of Walsingham, but they will rejoice that they are united with their brethren everywhere in their love for Mary, Queen of all Mankind. The Italians will cherish with sentimental affection Our Lady of Pompei and Our Lady of Loreto, but, on the level of their doctrinal thought and devotional loyalty, they will remember that she is the Queen of all Mankind.

And so the problem which chiefly worries us in the world of our day, the problem of these terrible divisions which tear at human unity and destroy the possibility of peace, will be met in the Age of Mary by an understanding of the universal queenship of Our Lady, the

Blessed Mother of the Universal Redeemer and Reconciler of all nations, all tribes, all classes, and all peoples.

From the ancient evil of the flesh our modern times have acquired as their besetting worry the contemporary cult of the human body, the quest of physical strength for its own sake, the admiration, indeed the adoration, of mere sensual beauty. Our times are plagued by literal heresies which arise from the cult of the physical and the love of the body: heresies on the political level like the heresy of Nazism with its pagan cult of blood; heresies on the esthetic level like the worship of the human form, the pagan cult of beauty; heresies on the scientific or pseudoscientific level like the health cults, the perverse religions of health which are contemporary expressions of the pagan cult of mere physical strength. In such an age the Church offers Mary assumed into heaven, body and soul integrated for all eternity, as a reminder of the true sanctity of the body, of the true dignity and the true beauty of human flesh as the spouse of the spirit, the servant of the soul, and the instrument of God, a means to the doing of the work of God.

Finally, from the devil in our modern age there comes the specific temptation of our times. The devil speaks to each generation in the terms most likely to seduce it. To one generation the devil speaks in terms of glory, to another in terms of conquest, to all in terms of pride. What is the principal approach which Satan makes in order to tempt our modern generation of Christian believers, and, specifically, of Catholics?

Our generation is too cynical to be seduced by promises of glory and magnificent victories. Wherefore I venture the opinion that the devil speaks to us in terms of worry. He tempts us with the spirit of defeatis-

and discouragement in the face of the titanic political, military, economic, social, and other worries of our day.

And so Mary, prefigured of old as the Woman who would crush the head of the serpent and cheat Satan of his victory, in our modern times must also help powerfully to correct the universal discouragement of the good, the sense of defeatism in believers, the plague of worry in the hearts of those who love God. In order to rouse our flagging spirits in a generation where Satan attempts to seduce believers by defeatism, discouragement, and worry, the Church offers us Mary of the *Magnificat*.

Have you ever wondered what point the providence of God might have in the timing of these definitions which come from the Church concerning the Blessed Mother? Why would it have been reserved for our times that the dogma of the Immaculate Conception, for example, should have been defined in our day rather than in another? I think that with a little meditation you will see that the Spirit of God arranges these things, so to speak, in order that the needed definition will be timed to meet the specific temptation of the hour. In our day of so many victories of organized malice and military might, the temptation is to believe that we are powerless, that we are too weak to prevail, that we are not merely a "tiny flock", as the Gospel described the Christian flock to be, but that we are an inconsequential, impotent flock with only pessimism as our prospect.[1]

And then the Holy Spirit of God impels the teaching Church to put before us the figure of the Immaculate Conception. As Cardinal Newman points out, in the figure of the Immaculate Conception we have a sure ion of what human nature is when it is free from sin

84

and therefore a vision of the beauty and strength of the nature we ourselves possess when finally we dominate by God's grace the sin which cripples it. Cardinal Newman wrote beautifully of the Immaculate Conception and its lessons for us, discouraged by our own weakness. He asked us to suppose that Eve had stood the trial instead of succumbing to the temptation, to suppose that she had kept the grace that was hers and ours in the beginning, and then to suppose that she eventually had children. Those children from the first moment of their existence would, through divine bounty, have received the same privileges that Eve had possessed. As she was taken from Adam's side clothed, so to say, in a garment of grace, so her children in turn would have received what may be called an *immaculate conception*. We, her descendants, would have been conceived in grace as in fact we are conceived in sin.

Mary is placed before our eyes as a daughter of Eve unfallen, and thus she shows us what our nature would have possessed supernaturally and by privilege if Eve had not fallen. When we speculate on this in these days of discouragement it should occur to us that, although we do not have the privileges that were Mary's or that were Eve's, nonetheless ours is still the nature that was elevated in Eve. It is deprived but not depraved, wounded but not intrinsically corrupted. Ours is the same human nature that Mary possessed and, therefore, in the splendor of Mary we have a promise of something of what we yet may be if we cooperate with the grace of God that is restored to us, but was hers from the beginning.

Then we should understand a little better why the Church in these troubled times salutes Mary as Cause of

Our Joy. It is not only because she brought into the world the Christ who opens up to us the treasures of grace but also because in her human nature she exemplified what grace accomplishes. She is the Cause of Our Joy and therefore in troubled times she inspires us to optimism rather than leaves us in pessimism.

The great ages of faith were joyful and gay, golden and bright blue like the paintings of Fra Angelico because they so readily turned their attention from what human nature is at its worst to what human nature is at its highest and best, as in the immaculately conceived Mother of Christ. So I bid you also do in these days so discouraged, so pessimistic. Lift up your eyes to Mary. Meditate frequently on the doctrines that Holy Church, in such timely and providential fashion, has put before our eyes in these modern days. Think of the Immaculate Conception and the Assumption of the Blessed Mother in terms of what these tell us concerning our own nature, the destiny of our race, and our own spiritual dignity.

Meditating on these mysteries, you will be stirred by nostalgic memories of what we humans were when the world was young and we walked in the Garden of God before our fall in Adam. Then you will be strengthened and encouraged in the hope of what we yet may be, certainly in heaven but in some degree on earth, when we have prayed in Our Mother, Our Queen, but also our sister in humanity, and thus have become worthy of the promises of Christ.

VII

Our Lady of Space

We stand on the shores of space. Events of recent months have impelled, more and more, the gaze of men outward beyond the skies, the stars, and all the space between. What mysteries for the scientist all this involves! What problems for the diplomat and the military tactician! What wonders for the theologian and the poet!

Thus far the scientist has had the most to say. The Geophysical Year, 1957–1958, has found him bursting with ideas and busy with projects, all focused on outer space. The diplomat and the military tactician, more nervous and less certain, have been scarcely less vigilant in their watching of the skies. While the scientist has been speaking to us of satellites, space ships, space medicine, and rockets, the diplomat and the statesman have begun to worry about sovereignty in space. A brief article on this problem has already appeared to tell us that political and strategic considerations have, indeed, provided the greatest single incentive to the development of rockets and space research and that the difficult question of sovereignty in space must now receive serious attention!

The devout understand that the earth is the Lord's and so are the heavens, so for them the radical problem of sovereignty in space is already largely solved.[1] But if the scientist, the statesman, and the military tactician are

This article was written for and published in the July–August 1958 issue of *Marist Missions*.

looking so eagerly out toward space, what must be the yearning with which the theologian, fired with however little imagination, must gaze into the firmament which so long has spoken to him of God and His majesty?[2] And with him, how eager must be the devout poet, who follows along behind the theologian, sometimes blurring, sometimes neatly matching, the theologian's footsteps.

One thinks of Plunkett's *Christ in the Universe* and Meynell's intriguing conception of the Incarnation renewed in worlds beyond our ken, and one realizes what a wealth of imaginative meditation awaits the devout poet as the theologians begin to interpret what the scientists are beginning to tell us of the worlds and universes which form all the creation scattered through boundless space!

We stand on the shores of space. Already not only the eyes of imagination but those of sense pierce beyond the margins of the cozy little world that once we knew. What shall we find out in that vast realm that sometimes seems so empty? Shall we find God? A naive, somewhat crude Soviet bulletin assures us we shall not. It says that nowhere along the minor way its rockets coursed could it find the slightest trace of the Christ of the Ascension! Some cosmic dust, perhaps; the orbit of their own dead dog. But no trace of God.

As we search higher or deeper or further—what does one say of journeys into space?—shall we one day encounter the Risen Christ or His Mother or His kingdom?

Christians know better. The visible universe, however vast, is one thing; the invisible universe, the realm of grace transcending nature, is quite another. Even before men began to talk of the distant reaches beyond the stars, knew that heaven lies all about us. We understand that it involves another dimension, say better another order, this other world in which one day we shall encounter and, please God, enjoy the life of the world to come.

Meanwhile, we know that it is we ourselves, the devout impelled by a missionary spirit akin to that which brought Christ out of the invisible world into the visible, out of heaven into history, out of eternity into time, that spirit which impels us to bring to the further corners of the visible order the tokens and influence of the world invisible.

So when the New World was opening up to exploration by the Irish and Norse missionaries a thousand years ago, or by the intrepid Latins a half century ago, the things that tell of God, of His Christ, His Mother, and His kingdom were brought by these devout souls to corners of the globe which were then as empty of reminders of Christ's kingdom as now the moon and all of space may be. It was their love for the Blessed Mother, for example, conceived in Spain or Italy or the Land of the North, that prompted them to bring into the remote, desolate places, the deserts, arctic regions, and desolate mountain heights, the name and the love of Our Lady of the Desert, Our Lady of the Snows, Our Lady of the Mountains. Wherever the knowledge of God has been present, carried in the minds of men, the tokens of the things of God have speedily followed.

One thinks of these things when, in the midst of the primeval solitudes, he suddenly comes upon Our Lady of the Saguenay, high on the cliffs above the river where the devout had placed her to remind future travelers in those lonely regions of how those who first penetrated the unknown brought with them the knowledge and love of Christ and His Mother. One thinks of these truths when he comes upon lakes in the wilderness of the remote Americas and finds there that those who came before him, centuries ago, as explorers or adventurers, gave her name to the lakes, the rivers, or other lovely places which they knew would one day delight other wanderers as the thought of her reflection of heaven had delighted them.

So as men prepare for journeys into outer space we are reminded (if only by the picayune complaints of the cantankerous who complain of Saint Christopher medals!) that among those who are planning the rockets which will soar out into space there are many devout men eager to bring tokens of the saints, of Christ, and His Blessed Mother wherever their own imagination, ingenuity, and energy may eventually penetrate. It is inevitable that these will speak to us of Our Lady of Space—and it is well.

We know so little, so pathetically little, of the galaxies, worlds, and universes which comprise creation. We know, at least, in our present state of knowledge only that Christ entered our world to redeem it and sanctify those who dwell within it. Everything that pertains to that world was touched by the hallowing influence of Christ, and as Scotus and Bonaventure tentatively tried to tell us, everything in the universe of which we are part is somehow bound up with Christ, recapitulated in Him, and through Him brought back to God. So far as our own universe, however tiny, however vast, is concerned, we know that it is made a temple, not a tomb, because of the living and radiant presence within it of the Spirit of God. The Little Flower understood this with an intuition at once poetic and theological. Christ remains supreme throughout our visible universe, and where Christ is, there is His kingdom and there must be its Queen.

The devout have long sensed how Mary is the Queen, not only of our dusty little globe in the visible order and of heaven in the invisible order of the life of the world to come, but also of the vast expanse of the universe within which our earth rolls on its way through space and of the soaring skies which speak to us of heaven.

In the Litany the devout have long called out to Mary as the *Morning Star*, giving her a place among the celestial wonders to which we lift up our eyes in hope and longing.[3] The hymns of seafaring Catholic Christians traditionally salute her as *Bright Star of the Ocean*, spiritually as bound up with our security and safety as is the polestar with the accuracy of our navigation.[4] The Sacred Scripture tells of the "woman clothed with the sun, and the moon under her feet, and upon her head a crown of twelve stars"![5] True, scholars tell us the reference is to the Church, but it is one of the references in Sacred Scripture which devout accommodation finds consistent with the glory of Mary. So is the line from the Old Testament, which the liturgy uses to sing her privileges, which tells of her who was brought forth before the daystar and made a part of God's blueprint for our creation.[6]

Our Lady of Space! Surely it is no accident that, as the world of science was preparing for its excursion beyond the familiar boundaries of the physical universe, the world of theology, headed by and speaking through the Vicar of Christ, should have been hailing the Blessed Mother as Queen of the Universe—no longer of France alone, nor of Montserrat, nor of Walsingham, nor o

Lourdes merely, nor of Guadalupe, Loreto, Vilna, Kazan, or China, nor even of all mankind—but of the world, the sun, the moon, and all the stars, as well as the space between.

Queen of the Universe, pray for us in this space age!

VIII

Mary and Christian Unity

Perhaps it needed the evils of two World Wars and the threat of world atheism to dispose the worldwide company of those who love God to seek the recovery of that social unity in which God created mankind from the beginning and the achievement of that supernatural unity, in one Lord and one faith, which the new Adam died to bring to pass.

If so, then history may yet decide not only that God has drawn good out of evil but also that the social and religious blessings of humanity, united after centuries of fratricidal division, far exceed in proportionate goodness all the appalling evils of the wars and the threats of revolution which will have helped us to our senses.

At all events, in these recent years the yearnings of Christendom for its own reunion have been increasingly ardent. All the logic of our times has favored such yearnings, and our darkest temporal and spiritual anxieties, as well as our fairest social and religious hopes, have tended to intensify the nostalgia for human unity which more and more characterizes our generation.

In the secular order there has been renewed emphasis on the supranational, universal, and humanitarian elements of civilization, and this after a long era of powerful nationalist, imperialist, and racist and related commitments of divided mankind. On the spiritual level devout

This sermon was preached at Saint Procopius Abbey, Lisle, Illinois, on July 1, 1959.

persons in every corner of the world are asking themselves how their particular religious traditions harmonize with the universal religious destiny of mankind, and thoughtful men seem disposed, as perhaps never before, to listen for the echoes of God's single, transcendent voice in the midst of the divided, discordant voices of the prophets of manmade religions.

Within Christendom, sensitive Protestants, among the good people in the denominations which have separated from Catholic Unity but retain the Christian name and aspirations, have begun to speak less of the differences which divide them from Catholicism and among themselves and to speak more of those ecumenical hopes which have been born of their new and divinely inspired yearnings for *world faith and order*. On every side Christians with profound understanding of what it is to be a follower of Christ are seeking unity in Christ, recognizing, as eventually all must do, that the tragic divisions within the Christian flock reflect man's willfulness rather than God's will.

Meanwhile, sympathy between the devout of the Eastern Orthodox churches and the faithful who have remained in communion with the successor to Peter as Vicar of Christ is greater than it has been in centuries. Despite political persecutions which still seek to impede such unity in faith and charity, the Uniate Catholics, wherever in the world they may be, rejoice as never before in their ties with the Holy See, and yet between them and their Orthodox brethren one notes with joy a loving understanding and fraternal forbearance which can only have come from grace and must assuredly herald greater graces yet to come.

And now, from the apostolic watchtower of the Holy

See there comes the thrilling call of Pope John XXIII for the Ecumenical Council. Such a council, while it may not solve all or even most of the problems in the way of Christian unity, certainly symbolizes the sure direction of all devout desires in our day, and even the most reserved reactions from outside the fold of Peter have dramatized how unity, ever the actual mark of the Church linked by Christ to Peter, has now become the ideal aspiration of all who acknowledge Christ as the Universal Redeemer and Divine Teacher of mankind.

Divine piety and human prudence caution against unduly sanguine expectations concerning the measure of the unity desired by Christ which will be attained as a result of widespread ecumenical hopes in our day, but there are nonetheless good grounds for holy, humble confidence as we now pray for the reunion of Christendom. One of these grounds, the more pertinent and impressive because it involves doctrine concerning Christ Himself, always the living cornerstone of Christian unity, is the consoling degree to which common doctrine and devotion still make the Mother of Christ a bond of faith and charity between the Catholic and Eastern Orthodox followers of her Son.

One cannot yet speak of the privileges of Mary as Mother of God without fear of alienating yet further many of our Protestant Christian brethren, but, as we reflect on those things which may bring together Orthodox Christians with their Catholic brethren, we can and must speak of the manner in which the doctrines and cult surrounding the Blessed Mother intensify that unity among us made possible by, with, and in Christ.

The doctrine of Mary as *Theotokos* and devotion to the Virgin under this sublime title have always been bonds between East and West. This doctrine of the divine maternity, the mystery that the Mother of Christ is the Mother of God, is veiled in wonder and eludes our human understanding. But it does so only because it is bound up with mysteries no less shrouded in the same wonder and elusive for the same reasons, above all the mystery, unmistakably true but beyond our power to tell, that Mary's Son is at once true God and true man. Saint Cyril's account of why Mary is properly called *Theotokos* summarized the teaching East and West have steadfastly shared:

> Therefore the Word indeed was God, but He became also man; and because He was born according to the flesh, because of His humanity, it is necessary that she who gave birth to Him should be the Mother of God. For if she did not give birth to God, certainly neither will He be called God Who was begotten of her. But if the divine Scriptures call Him God, she then gave birth to God made man because a man could not otherwise come to be except through generation from a woman. How then is not she who bore Him the Mother of God? That He is true God Who was born of her, we learn from the divine Scripture.

But there is a further understanding concerning the Blessed Mother which East and West should explore together and which provides further strong grounds for our common cult and increased unity: This further understanding pertains to Mary's spiritual maternity. As mother of Christ, Mary is somehow also mother of mankind. If by begetting Christ and bringing Him into the world Mary became the mother of God, so by the same maternity she became not only the mother of the Redeemer but the mother of the redeemed. Her maternity links her through Christ to God but also through Christ to us. Here, too, the place of Mary in the total economy of salvation is given focus, and the nature of the privileged relations between the devout and Divinity are clarified. By grace we are the children of God, the brethren of Jesus. In the mystery of that grace we are assimilated to Christ in a supernatural life which gives us a supernatural relationship to Mary and gives her a relationship to us. The mother of my Redeemer is somehow my mother, too. Saint Stanislas Kostka loved to repeat a claim consistent with the strictest Catholic theological accuracy and comprehensible to every Orthodox mind and heart: "The Mother of God is my mother."

Here, too, is mystery profound and ineffable, but the mystery, again, surrounds how these wonders can be, not whether and what they are. When we speak of the spiritual maternity of Mary, of the Mother of Christ as the mother of all redeemed, we speak a mystery, but we are not without insights to help us understand the mystery. These insights, we pray, will be studied together by Orthodox and Catholic theologians so that all who adore Christ and venerate His Mother may be brought closer to one another because of their understanding of something, at least, of what we mean by the marvelous titles that Eastern and Western Christians have not hesitated to give the Blessed Virgin, all of which derive from the central, supreme fact that she is the Mother of Christ.

Reflections on the Blessed Mother and on the unity we have with her and with one another in, through, and because of Christ will nourish the desire for unity and will link that desire to its necessary dogmatic basis. For our human nostalgia for unity stems from the solidarity that once mankind had in Adam, while our divinely implanted desire for supernatural unity with one another and with God comes from the grace merited for us by Him through Whom and in Whom our reunion can alone be achieved, the new Adam Who is Christ Jesus.

The relation of the spiritual maternity of Mary to all these mysteries is suggested by Pope Benedict XV when he hails Mary as the new Eve, the spiritual mother of redeemed mankind, as Eve was the physical mother of our race.

> For as the first Adam had a woman as his associate in the Fall, so the second Adam willed that there participate in the reparation of our salvation she whom, by styling her "Woman" from the Cross, He declared to be the second Eve, that is, the ineffable sorrowing mother of all men, for whom He was dying, to win life for them.

God grant that, as we become more conscious of whose children we are, we may more joyfully recognize one another as brethren. For we are no longer merely the creatures of God but His sons and daughters, the brothers and sisters of His incarnate Son. "To as many as received Him, He gave the power to become the sons of God; for they are born, not of the blood nor of the will of the flesh nor of the will of man, but of God."[1] So we, one in Christ, are spiritually and supernaturally brethren in a family, the intimacy of which the world of sense cannot even guess. We are no longer Easterners or Westerners, save only in cherished secondary traditions, but are one people of God, thanks to the redemptive action of the new Adam and our ties in grace with the new Eve.

IX

The Third Word from the Cross

Now there stood by the Cross of Jesus, His Mother
and His Mother's sister, Mary of Cleophas, and Mary
Magdalen. When therefore Jesus had seen His Mother
and the disciple standing there whom He loved, He said
to His Mother: "Woman, behold thy son." After that,
He said to the disciple: "Behold thy mother." And from
that hour, the disciple took her into his home.[1]

We turn now from sinners to saints, from those who
cannot yet be rid of Christ, though they hate Him, to
those who are free to leave Him but will not because they
love Him more than life itself. Does it not seem strange
to you that the first thought of Jesus should have been for
His murderers, taking the form of an anxiety lest they be
punished for the crimes they were doing against Him?[2]
That His second thought should have been for a man
who was, in one sense, a total stranger and that only
when He had comforted this poor thief did He think of
His own flesh and blood, His Mother, and of the disciple
whom most especially He cherished as His friend?[3]

Does it disturb you? Before you answer that to you it
does *not* seem strange, think hard! Do even you, who are
Catholics, sometimes find it inhuman when a young
boy leaves home and fatherland to offer himself as a
missionary, to preach the kingdom of God to nations
who, denying Christ, still know not what they do? Or
when a lovely girl, fresh and high-spirited, immures

This conference, on the third of the seven last words of Christ, was
preached in 1960, at Saint Paul Cathedral, Pittsburgh, Pennsylvania

herself in a convent to offer her life, her days and nights of prayer, for thieves unknown and sinners unloved, that they too may one day be with Christ in paradise? Does it not seem strange that they should (so far as outward actions go) think first of those who hate them, or of those whom they do not even know, and only then find time for parents and friends and lovers?

God has always acted this way with those whom He loves and that Christ should so act is another manifestation of the divinity of Him Who died on Calvary. God has always expected His saints to act in this way, and that the finest flower of His Church should so act is another proof of the identity with Christ of that Church which seems, even at times to its members, so strange and so inhuman in its demands.

We have seen the majestic dignity of Jesus on His Cross. Perhaps it would be well here to remind ourselves that human sentiments, even human tears, were not inconsistent with the divine dignity of the Lord. The Scriptures recount that three times in His life Our Lord wept, but no tears of merely physical pain or personal frustration were these tears of Jesus. He wept for love of His friend at the tomb of Lazarus; He wept for love of His nation, gazing upon the doomed city of Jerusalem; He wept for love of God at the thought of the evil that brought Him to Calvary.

These last tears His Blessed Mother, adding tears for Him, shared on Calvary. But the tears of Mary, we must believe, are no less noble than those of her sacred Son whom she mirrored faithfully. In her, on Calvary, we may expect to find the fortitude and the majesty with which Jesus Himself drank the cup of sorrows to its utter emptying.

No one who knows mothers has been responsible for the tradition of the fainting Mother of Sorrows whom we encounter in so many pietistic paintings and books of baroque devotion. No one who has ever seen other mothers, far less perfect than she, take leave of their own flesh and blood at sailings for distant exile, at the departure of troop trains, at open graves, can quite accept the picture of Mary which these provide. Men marvel at the strength of the mother of the persecuted Maccabees, and they recognize other mothers in that valiant woman of whom the Scriptures tell:

> She was to be admired above measure, and worthy to be remembered by all good men, who beheld her seven sons slain in one day and bore it with good courage, for the hope that she had in God; and she bravely exhorted every one of them to remain faithful, being filled with wisdom and joining a man's heart to a woman's thoughts.[4]

Remembering these other mothers, we are relieved to find in the Gospels no hint of unbecoming grief in Mary, no word of moral or physical shrinking in that mother whom Catholics hail as their advocate and their strength. Mary espoused the redemption in silence; she did not cry out; she is not named among the women who wept for her Son. We read in the Gospel only these movingly restrained words: "Now there *stood* by the Cross of Jesus His Mother."[5] "I read that she stood," says Saint Ambrose, "I read nowhere that she wept." Yet . . . tears there doubtless were, silent tears, noble tears, tears like those of Christ whose co-sufferer she was.

Mary, despite her great grace and singular intimacy with Jesus, was still utterly human. Closely intimate was her knowledge of Christ; still she walked by faith in Hi divinity, a faith unmatched among men, but faith no less than ours. We must not forget how different, as well as how alike, were the sufferings of Jesus and Mary. Now that His hour had come, Jesus, consoled by the Beatific Vision, the clear knowledge of God's goodness and God's truth which never ceased entirely to irradiate His human mind, could exult in His most agonizing sorrows at the thought of the early harvest of grace and glory which His sufferings would win. Mary, though, sustained by faith more ardent than ever before, must have found herself on Calvary fighting fears more harrowing than she had ever known as she stood by the Cross of Jesus and gazed on flesh of her flesh, naked as the day she bore Him, mangled beyond a mother's power to heal.

The measure of Mary's grief is the measure of her love; and we who cannot equal the purity of the love of Mary for Jesus cannot realize the agony which the sight of His sufferings caused her. She loved Him as her own familiar friend because of the long and loyal common life she had shared with Him. She loved Him as a disciple might love an incomparable master for the sublime teaching she had received from Him. She loved Him as a perfect mother must love a son perfect in soul and beautiful in body. She loved Him as the Queen of all martyrs must love the God and Redeemer for whom countless martyrs, without ever seeing Him, have been willing to die and for whom countless Christian maidens, merely for having heard His name, have been willing all the days of their lives to imitate the virginity of His Mother.

What must this daughter of Eve have suffered who, ving Jesus by these titles we can scarcely understand

and with an intensity we can never measure, gathered together within the narrow space of a woman's fragile heart all the martyrdoms and all the torments which were dispersed over the body of Jesus, her Son! Even a mother, in order to appreciate Mary's affliction, would have to be as sensitive, because as pure, as Mary; as devoted, because as close to Jesus. Yet only a mother may even guess the sorrow of Mary on Calvary.

But perhaps a man, a son, can feel something of the sympathy of Jesus for His Mother. Outraged and dishonored, He saw the last person in the world who would wish for Him this end gazing upon Him with unflinching loyalty. The sight of her reminded Him of past joys; in her grief she stood with women with whom she had once shared the happiness she found in Him, but women who now, far less than she, could hope to comprehend the mystery of iniquity which seemed to have brought Him—and His Mother—to infamous confusion. He saw all pale and wasted that face once so like His own that just as He is called the Sun of Justice, so she is called its mirror. Hands which once had lifted Him, He saw now impotent to take Him down; hands which once had opened, simply and graciously, to greet Him, He saw now dry and twisted from unconscious clenching. Bent was the ivory tower of her queenly body, trembling the mystic rose of her virginal mouth, taxed to the limits of its endurance by a mother's compassion was her maternal courage. And seeing her pathetic efforts to share His dignity who shared His suffering, Jesus wept for His blessed mother.

O Jesus Christ, true Son of God and perfect Man, as sincerely as ever we thanked Thee for all the gifts of Thy creation, for all the graces of Thy redemption, we thank Thee for Thy tears. Never again shall we be ashamed to weep for those we love! Never shall we regret that we are as human as God's own Son—human. He, even at the apex of a work which only His divinity could do! Every tear that the innocent have shed in exile, every tear that the loving have shed in separation, every tear that a human being has shed in sorrow, in bewilderment —not Mary alone, but Jesus consecrated on Calvary when tears of Mary's Son mingled with blood that belonged to God in the laver that cleansed and redeemed us.

X

Our Lady of Guadalupe

I must begin by expressing my prayerful, warm gratitude for the extraordinarily beautiful chalice I received from The Mariological Society of America on the recent occasion of my Silver Sacerdotal Jubilee. The exquisite chalice is the work of the fervent and affectionate imagination of our dynamic spur to all good deeds within the Society, Father Juniper Carol; it will be treasured as the most significant and welcome of all possible souvenirs of my priestly years, combining, as it does, the symbols of Mary, the memory of beloved saints, the pledge of your prayers, and the vessel essential to the daily liturgy.[1]

It is, then, with added motives of grateful appreciation that I bid you all welcome this morning. I beg God's blessing on your deliberations and pray that they will contribute mightily to the refreshment of the thought, work, and devotion of all our Mariologists.

I note with special satisfaction that theme of your deliberations. It links the Old Testament hopes with the New Testament realities and invites you, as specialists in studies on the Blessed Mother, to make your contribution to the strengthening of the ties, intellectual and spiritual, between all the heirs to Hebrew prophecy and the disciples of Christian preaching concerning the kingdom of Christ and the privileges of His Blessed Mother.

Permit me to add a comment of a topical and de-

Message to the 1961 convention of the American Mariological Society.

votional character. Pope John XXIII has declared a Marian Year for Mexico to commemorate the fiftieth anniversary of the proclamation by Pope Saint Pius X of the patronage of Our Lady of Guadalupe for all the Latin American countries.

The Marian Year runs from October 12, 1960, to October 12, 1961. These dates are also significant, for October 12 is the civil holiday honoring the opening up by Columbus of the New World to European colonization and to the preaching by Catholic missionaries of the Christian faith. The great admiral sailed the seas on a flagship bearing the name of Mary; his daily prayer and that of his devout men was: "Jesus cum Maria sit nobis in via!"[2]

The Mexican Marian Year and the devotion to Our Lady of Guadalupe are of direct concern to Latin America. But I venture the strong suggestion that we of the United States and Canada have an intimate interest in both. It becomes daily, perhaps one should say *hourly*, more clear that the destinies of all the Americas are inextricably intertwined; the sources of evil for all the nations of both American continents are the same, and so must be the sources of inspiration and strength. We of the United States and Canada owe it to ourselves and to our Latin American brethren to lose the advantage of nothing that will make us more surely and more securely united in love for the Catholic faith and in defense of our freedom to profess and practice that faith.

I think it exact to say that the first major threat to such faith and freedom to come from the modern specifically atheistic revolution was that which struck Mexico so cruelly in the 1920s. By the same token, I think it significant that the first successful resistance to aggressive atheism in a nation of the Americas was that of the Catholic Mexicans of the land favored by the apparitions and first patronage of Our Lady of Guadalupe.

The fresh menace of the same spirit of atheistic revolution to the Catholic faith and human freedom all over America, beginning in Latin America but by no means confined to there, makes it, I think, timely and urgent that I preface your academic, scholarly sessions by a plea that you watch for opportunities in your teaching, writing, and preaching to stimulate devotion to Our Lady of Guadalupe during the Mexican Marian Year and during all the period of grave menace to Catholicism and to civilization.

XI

Eve, Mary, and the Modern Woman

The growing lay retreat movement among Catholic women focuses attention on three personalities—Eve, Mary, and the modern woman.[1]

All that we know about Eve we know from a few obscure and fugitive phrases in the first pages of the Old Testament. These few phrases, most of them not even sentences, and a couple of corollaries from theological speculation about revealed truths give the few clues on which we must depend for knowledge of the personality and the circumstances of Eve.

The basic truth about Eve is summed up in her name. That name we receive from the Hebrews and, we are told, it meant to them *the mother of all the living*. But what do we know of the personality of this mother of all the living? Well, we know that she was all that a woman would be, fresh from the hand of the God of Love Who created her. In the freshness of the beginning of things she had about her the beauty of a perfect creature divinely planned, newly made by the hand of God Himself. That tells us something of the dignity, the majesty, and the graciousness—the *gracefulness* in every sense—that must have been hers, physically, mentally, spiritually, naturally, and supernaturally.

What do we know of her circumstances, the conditions under which Eve found herself? These, too, are

This address was delivered before the Peoria Council of Catholic Women on September 10, 1961.

108

summed up in the single word by which the Scripture describes the world she lived in. It is called a garden—the Garden of Eden—paradise. This, too, is only a phrase, but it speaks to us eloquently of how beautiful must have been the world when Eve, fresh from the hand of God and the privileged object of His loving providence and creative power, first saw the dawn, the sky, and all things that are.

We can reason, too, to some idea of what must have been her beauty, majesty, and loveliness from what we know of her daughters, even in their fallen state and after centuries of aberration, decadence, and degeneration from the ideal that was Eve. We know the power they still retain to inspire, to ennoble, to make paradiselike even what is left of Eden on earth. Reasoning from these shattered remnants of what her perfection must have been, these ashlike evidences of their original prototype's gifts, we can form some dim idea of the nobility, the majestic dignity, and the grace of Eve.

We are told of one of her daughters, Helen of Troy, that men burned one another's cities and risked their own lives, dying ignominious deaths, merely at the thought that after their deaths their cities might claim her as queen. How beautiful Helen must have been! And yet she was born after generations of the decadence of that human nature which was perfect in Eve.

We know of other queens—Cleopatra, for instance—that emperors went mad for the desire of them. If this was their allure, even after centuries of degeneration from the original beauty of our race, what must have been the majesty of Eve? We know Mary Stuart—that she was a weak and sinful woman, a pathetically weak daughter of Eve, with only traces ever so vestigial of the majesty and the dignity of Eve. Yet the reflection of her broken beauty made Elizabeth mad with jealousy and so captivated Ronsard that he remembered it in his sonnets years later. From her we can guess something of what must have been the beauty of Eve—spiritual, mental, and physical—centuries before, when womanhood, like the world itself, was new.

And yet, for all that beauty, majesty, and graciousness, we remember Eve as the mother of our tears, the cause of our grief. She is not merely the mother of all the living; she is quite literally the mother of all the damned, the mother of all the brokenhearted, the mother of our sorrows.

What made her so? Was it the place in which she lived? Was it any circumstances of environment? Her dwelling place was described as a garden—paradise. Was the world about us so different then from what it is now? Was the sun in a different place? It wasn't. Did the moon follow any different course? It didn't. Weren't the stars in the same tracks then in which they ride now? Weren't the mountains then as they are now—and fields, valleys, lakes, and rivers? They must have been. It is in their nature that they should have been. When Eve dwelled among them, fresh from the hand of God, they constituted paradise. Now we are terrified of them. What made the difference in it all?

It was something in *her*. She had within her the power to change herself and therefore to change *them*, at least in their relation to her and to us. She exercised that power. She turned the Garden of Eden into a valley of tears—a place in which, mourning and weeping, we seek to work out our salvation.

The few fugitive phrases of Scripture which tell us

about Eve are chiefly the phrases which suggest to us—only suggest—the process by which she changed all things, beginning with herself. The phrases are few, I repeat, and obscure, but this is the line of reasoning that they suggest.

Eve looked about her and she found all things paradisal. She looked within herself and found all things sublime—mind, spirit, personality—all perfection. They were not only endowed with the perfection of their nature but superadded to them was a perfection just short of God-like. There was the rub! She had all things, but she was *beholden* for them. She knew all secrets, certainly all consistent with felicity and perfection, but all that she had and all that she knew, including the very power to have and to know, she owed to another. She did not have these of herself.

And so, serpent-like, there was insinuated into Eve's reflections on her condition and on herself the thought that, although she possessed perfection and paradise itself, still there was conceivable a state even more to be preferred. Such would be the same state that she possessed but not dependent on the good pleasure of another. If only she could have what she already possessed but might have these of herself, so that she need say "Thank you" to nobody, then she would be happier. And so the temptation came: "How do you rejoice in this paradise which is yours to enjoy, when you did not make it? How can you rejoice in these gifts which make you majestic and sublime, when you are not their origin? You will have to render an account for your use of them and this subordinates you. Would you be as God, not only possessing good things but determining what *is* good and what *isn't*? Would you not rather have these things, which are now yours, but have them by your own *right*, as now only God has things, being no longer answerable to anyone outside yourself, not even to God, but only answerable to your own godlike good pleasure? If you would be as gods, exercise your right and revolt. Since freedom is of the essence of your human perfection, proclaim a declaration of independence and assert your answerability only to yourself."

And thus it was, so that paradise became what we daily see about us and what, more painfully still, we daily and nightly see *within* us. All is changed.

We turn in meditation now to the new Eve—to Mary, the Mother of Jesus. What do we know of her? As a matter of biographical record, we know relatively little. All that we know we know again from a few fugitive phrases, not so obscure and much more recent, but still not very developed—the phrases in the first pages in the books of the New Testament.

Where do we find Mary as her story opens? What are her circumstances? Suffice it to say, they are not *summed* up in the words "a garden, a paradise". We read of her, in the first few phrases of the clues to her story, that she was the espoused wife of Joseph, a carpenter, and that she lived in towns, now here, now there, in Judea and Galilee, places in the land which we call *the Holy Land* largely because of her Son.

That she was the spouse of Joseph and that she lived in these places tells us how ungardenlike were the circumstances in which Mary found herself. If there is one word more than another which does *not* describe those circumstances, that word is "garden". Those who have visited these same places in our own day have left there with a sense of great disillusion and shock, not to say scandal, even after two thousand years of relative progress beyond the circumstances in which Mary found herself as the spouse of Joseph. If you live in a house which is within walking distance of running water, then in comfort and convenience you are a hundred-up on the palace of Solomon in its best days, and Solomon was a king. Mary was espoused to a *carpenter*.

If you visit those same countries now, if you visit the land out of which her people came and go down the roads from Jerusalem to the remote country towns which were the scenes of her life and work, then even the homes of captains and kings will repel you. The homes of workers will sicken you even *now*, and Mary lived in one two thousand years ago when she was espoused to Joseph.

And so we must not think of the physical circumstances of Joseph the Carpenter in terms of the modern advantages of those who work with their hands. You must not think of Nazareth in terms of any town you know or any place where you have ever been or where your ancestors have been in these last thousand years. And yet, isn't it curious? When we think of Mary, we do not picture things as the reality would require us to think of them even now—of dust and flies; of vermin, filth, and disorder; of confusion, bickering, and all the sordid life of a Middle Eastern town. Yet that is where she lived. We don't think of it that way at all. We think of it in terms of stained glass and marble, of porphyry, tapestry, beautiful backgrounds of green and verdant hills. We think of her as the great Italian artists of the late Middle Ages and the Renaissance thought of her, surrounded by fruit, flowers, and birds: the Madonna of the Bullfinch, the Madonna of the Pomegranate, the Madonna of the Apple, the Madonna of the many fruits of della Robbia, the Madonna in exquisite blue and gold of Fra Angelico, the Madonna of Correggio, the Madonna of Lippo Lippi. We think of her as surrounded by physical beauty of the most magnificent kind. But it wasn't that way at all!

She was espoused to a carpenter from a small town on the backroads of a part of the world where even today most people would be miserable in the best hotel. What, then? Are the painters lying when they paint her surrounded by beauty? Are the tapestry weavers deceiving us or are they themselves deceived when they cannot find threads golden enough to tell us how resplendent it all was? Are the composers mistaken when they give us glorious melodies which seek to recapture the wonder of it? Are they suffering from illusion about the realities of Nazareth and of Mary's home?

Not at all! It was every bit as bleak, as forbidding, as sordid, as filthy as fact tells us. And yet it was every bit as beautiful, as noble, as sublime as the paintings, the music, and the tapestries tell us—and all because *she* was there. The physical circumstances were abominable by any standard, and yet we remember it with sweetness, rejoicing, and songs of *Magnificat* simply because Mary was in the midst of it all and gave it spiritual splendor.

When we remember the Garden of Eden, it is with remorse from which no psychiatrist can loose us. Our confessions leave us still uneasy, and baptism itself does not destroy the traces of its evil fruit—and it was a garden. We remember it so because Eve was *there*,

114

ambitious, jealous, avaricious. Yet we remember dust heaps with poetry and as having been beautiful because Mary was *there*.

Curious, isn't it, that the line by which we remember Eve is "Ye shall be as gods", while the line by which we remember Mary is "Behold the handmaid of the Lord; be it done to me according to thy word"—*Ecce ancilla Domini*.[2]

Every woman is Eve; every one is also called to be Mary. Each has the power to turn paradise into hell, as did Eve, or to transform dreary Nazareth into the delights of the Italian paintings, the stained glass, and the marble in which we remember Mary with wistfulness, gratitude, and wonder.

Lay retreats are part, a most important part, of the Church's resources for disciplining the instincts of Eve and developing the pattern of Mary in the modern woman. The lay retreat house recreates something of the Garden of Peace that was in the beginning. It brings us back to something of that closeness to God in which our first parents walked when the world was young and we were God's friends.

A time of spiritual retreat poses to the modern woman the age-old question which was asked both of Eve and Mary. "Will you serve God or will you seek to compete with Him?" This is the question which Eve answered with "I shall be as God, setting my own standards of good and evil", and which Mary answered with "Behold the handmaid of the Lord; be it done to me according to thy word"![3]

The Retreat Movement helps every woman to understand how Mary in humility achieved the ambition which Eve lost in pride, how she became Godlike by the use of the freedom through which she perfectly fulfilled what our retreats teach all women to pursue—that will of God that we literally be as God, not in the sense that Satan meant, but as Christ intended when He said: "Be ye perfect as your Heavenly Father is perfect."[4]

That is why the Church is persuaded that the Retreat Movement, more than any single thing after the sacraments and prayer, turns Eve into Mary and the world into paradise.

XII

The Cult of Mary in
The Age of the Cult of the Flesh

Our Catholic faith and our consequent Catholic moral, ascetical, and spiritual teaching are replete, heavily influenced by the purity, the angelic virtue, the chaste spirituality of Mary. But the culture all around us, the civilization which we share with our generation, is once again filled with emphasis on the flesh and especially on the satisfaction, sometimes not only licentious but also violent, of the demands of the flesh. In its commercial advertising, its entertainment, its everyday living, our culture tends to exploit, to exaggerate, and to satiate the instincts of flesh.

Hence the need for a renewed theology concerning Mary, "our tainted nature's solitary boast", as the Protestant poet called her, the living personification of the highest ideals of chastity.[1] Hence the need for a Christian *theology concerning the flesh*, so that our culture may be refined by it, our civilization may be cured of excess and purified of decadence, our lives made sane and *holy* by it. The flesh must also be made sacred; human nature must never become mere flesh, least of all despiritualized, animal flesh.

This is one of the master problems of our times; it has always been a grave problem for believers in the spirit

This sermon was preached (in Italian) at the Basilica of Our Lady of Pompeii, Naples, Italy, on December 8, 1969.

117

who nonetheless must live by the flesh, for creatures of flesh who are called to live by the spirit, for humanity born of Adam and Eve but reborn by the grace of Jesus brought to us thanks to Mary.

Under her title of the *Mother of the Church*, the Virgin Mother of Christ and of all the redeemed most especially symbolizes and solves the problem of a theology of the flesh. The word flesh has suggestive overtones which strike a discordant note in the Marian theme that runs through our Catholic Litany: *Mary Most Pure*, *Mary Most Chaste*, *Mary Inviolate*.[2]

In an earlier age, the word had similar overtones and even more diabolical undertones. But it was precisely to free the word of such evil connotations that Saint John, in the prologue to his Gospel, chose the word *flesh* and no other to announce the mystery of the Incarnation wherein the "Word became flesh".[3] It was precisely to underscore the sanctity of the flesh that the earliest Christian creed closed with a profession of faith in the resurrection of the flesh. Today, there is an urgent need to reassert the sanctity of the flesh to free the very word from the morbid or half-evil connotation that surrounds it, to inspire the word with the reverence that it deserves. To this purpose we have decided to consider *Mary* and the *flesh* to suggest the relation of the cult of Mary and the great Marian dogmas to what may be called the theology of the flesh.

When we think of Mary's influence on the theology of the early Church, we usually begin with the Council of Ephesus, held in the year 431. Here, the divinity of Christ was upheld against Nestorius by an appeal to Mary's most privileged title, *Theotokos*, Mother of God.

And yet Mary's influence in controlling Christian teaching goes back to the very infancy of the Church, to those early years when the question, "What think ye of Christ?", was first put to the pagan.

It is in these early decades that we find a group called Docetists, on the fringe of the Christian community, which denied not so much the divinity of Christ as His humanity. Their name came from the Greek word *dokein*, to appear, to seem, to make believe. These earliest of heretics taught that Christ's body was but a phantom, that He only seemed to be born of a woman, that His suffering, death, and Resurrection were only make-believe. Strangely enough, the Docetists found it more credible that Christ should be in some sense a Son of God than that He should be the Son of Mary.

In the letters to the Christians at Ephesus and at Smyrna, Saint Ignatius reveals the basic problem that confronted the Docetists. It is the *scandal of the flesh*. That the Word should take flesh from a woman, that the Eucharist should perpetuate on earth the mystery of the Word enfleshed, that the flesh should be capable of the gift of immortality, such an exaltation or apotheosis of flesh was blasphemous to these protoheretics. Christians, writes Ignatius to the Ephesians, "must beware of them, for they are hard to cure. There is only one physician, both carnal and spiritual, born and unborn, God become man, true life in death, sprung both from Mary and from God; first subject to suffering and then incapable of it—Jesus Christ Our Lord."[4] And to the Smyrnaeans he writes: "From Eucharist and prayer they hold aloof because they do not confess that the Eucharist is the flesh of Our Savior Jesus Christ, which suffered for our sins and which the Father in His loving kindness raised from the dead."[5]

To the pagan the great stumbling block to an acceptance of Christianity was the *scandalum crucis*, *the scandal of the Cross*. To the Docetist Christians the great stone of stumbling was the *scandalum carnis*, *the scandal of the flesh*. That the Christian God was born of a woman's flesh was unthinkable. To the pagan and the Jew the great obstacle was the tomb. To the Docetist it was even more the womb. No wonder that the Church in her great hymn of praise, *Te Deum Laudamus*, addresses Christ: "Tu ad liberandum suscepturus hominem, non horruisti Virginis uterum"—Thou, when about to take man's deliverance, didst not draw back in horror of the Virgin's womb.[6]

This abhorrence of the flesh which runs through Docetist teaching was not something native to classical paganism. On the contrary, pagan mythology made indulgent sport of the carnal amours of its gods with mortals. The attitude underlying Docetism was of Eastern origin. Some five centuries before the Christian era, on the far eastern borders of Persia, or Iran, Zoroaster had spoken of the irreconcilable conflict between Light and Darkness, Spirit and Matter, Good and Evil.

In even more remote India, the Buddha Gautama had proclaimed his antagonism against the material universe and taught that peace could result only with its annihilation.

Just when this alien pessimism entered the Graeco-Roman world it is difficult to say, but it was already present when Christianity was first being preached, and it was destined to grow with Christianity as an ugly and sometimes infectious influence on Christians. How serious this rival philosophy or religion was is proved by the attention that the earliest Christian writers gave it. It is they who first gave it a name, and it is principally from them that we learn of its strange and even fantastic doctrines.

Gnosticism was the name given to this heresy. It had no necessary stigma, being derived from the Greek word *gnosis* which simply means knowledge but not that Christian knowledge which is based on faith and which leads to charity. It was a speculative knowledge, a knowledge which "puffeth up" with pride and a knowledge devoid of charity; it was cold intellectualism.

This element of pride is seen in the idea of one religion designed for the intellectuals and another for the ignorant masses. The Christian wisdom founded on faith was God's free gift to the simple and to the wise alike, to the unlettered as well as the lettered, to the weak even more than to the strong. For the Gnostic, wisdom was the fruit of man's own reasoning and could be possessed only by the elite, by men of intellect and refinement. Salvation by way of faith, informed by charity, was the goal set for the Christian; salvation by way of knowledge, *gnosis*, was the goal set for the Gnostic. The Gnostic's vocation was not to believe but to know.

All the Gnostics are not yet dead. They publish articles regularly and have renewed their theology for our generation and our age in the life of the Church.

Their basic dualism between faith and experience, between matter and spirit, between the soul and the flesh, which is common to almost every form of Gnosticism, had quite opposite results in the sphere of practical morality. In some, it manifested itself in an exaggerated asceticism which endeavored to mortify the flesh, to kill the flesh, in order to set the soul free of its imprisoning influence.

There has been a tendency among writers who do not fully understand Christian faith and spirituality to identify the asceticism of these extremists with the genuine Christian attitude toward marriage and the other good things of God's creation. Even when there is a surface similarity, the motives that prompted Gnostics and Christians to forego marriage, meat, wine, and property are wholly different. The Church praises renunciation, writes Epiphanius, but she does not condemn marriage; she preaches poverty but does not inveigh intolerably against those who possess property . . . many in the Church abstain from certain kinds of food but do not look with contempt upon those who do not so abstain.

Admittedly there were some Christians, clergy as well as laymen, who were prompted to a life of renunciation from motives more Gnostic than Christian. But the attitude of the Church toward such is revealed in the following disciplinary decree which dates back to the fourth century:

> If a bishop, priest, deacon, or any other member of the clergy abstains from marriage, flesh, meat, and wine from the motive of contempt and not from the motive of asceticism, he is unmindful of the fact that God made all, things exceedingly good, that He made man male and female. In his blasphemy he condemns creation; therefore let him be corrected or deposed and ejected from the Church; and the same applies to a layman.

Saint Paul was a celibate and he encouraged others to embrace the same kind of life, but he recognized that each one has his own gifts from God.[7] He recognized as well that the renunciation of marriage could be prompted by motives diabolical as well as divine, and it is against an incipient Gnosticism that Saint Paul warns Timothy:

> Now the Spirit expressly says that in after times some will depart from the faith, giving heed to deceitful spirits and doctrines of devils, speaking lies hypocritically, and having their consciences branded. They will forbid marriage and will enjoin abstinence from food which God has created to be partaken of with thanksgiving by the faithful and by those who know the truth. For every creature of God is good, and nothing is to be rejected that is accepted with thanksgiving. For it is sanctified by the word of God and prayer.[8]

There is, however, another aspect or phase of Gnostic morality which manifested itself in an unbridled licentiousness, a conscious effort to free oneself of the law of the flesh by flouting it. So long as the soul feasted on the true knowledge, or *gnosis*, it could not be defiled by so worthless a thing as the body or so inconsequential a thing as carnal sin. Like the more ascetical-minded of their confreres, they too would repudiate marriage lest they perpetuate the kingdom of darkness by imprisoning souls in the flesh, but there were other means of gratifying their lusts, and there is sufficient evidence in the history of every Gnostic group that they speedily found them.

It is this form of *emancipated* Gnosticism, of moral self-centered permissiveness in matters sexual—and therefore basic to carnal activity and theory—that is insurgent, indeed dominant, in our day, not only in areas of commerce and amusement but also of ideology, even in some *theologies*.

123

I shall not linger on historic perversions of Christian spirituality and consequent forgetting of Catholic truth concerning the dignity of human flesh or on the lessons concerning the perfection of Mary by the power of God, especially in what pertains to the relations between spirit and flesh in sound Christian doctrine. Suffice it to recall the errors of the Manicheans, against whom Saint Augustine waged intellectual battle; the excesses of the Albigensians, with their perverse theories of *perfection* and of Christian *fulfillment*; against these latter Saint Dominic preached specifically a fervent Catholic cult of Mary to emphasize at once the true primacy of the spirit and the dignity as well as beauty of the flesh.

This cult of Mary took the popular form, encouraged by Saint Dominic, of the beloved rosary, with its constant repetition of the *Ave Maria*: the salute of the angel of God to flesh full of grace, to flesh within fallen humanity, to a womb blessed by its fruit, the Son conceived by the Holy Spirit to become "true God of true God", who became *flesh* for us, for us who are flesh, and for our salvation, being born of the *flesh* of the Virgin Mary of the Immaculate Conception, a theology of the flesh.

I pass over the denial of the doctrine concerning Mary by many of the Protestant theologies of centuries gone by, and I merely mention the concomitant disdain of the flesh, which even extended to the sacred flesh of Christ, which, in fact, was one of the characteristics of many Protestant theological aberrations, as well as later Catholic deviations from faith and order.

Such forgetfulness of the humanity of Jesus and denial of the dignity of the flesh of Mary, somehow shared every redeemed Christian, made felt its pessimistic influence among Protestant Puritans and Catholic Jansenists. It led many to reject everything but the spirit—and that spirit badly understood—even to the point of condemning flesh as evil, the Church as mere institution, liturgy as sensual, oral prayer itself and the sacramental life as *concessions* to the flesh. Inevitably, such fury and nonsense led to reactions of libertinism—as Puritanism always does—and to a false cult of the flesh, undisciplined by revolt against order rather than enjoyed in the freedom that comes from truth.

So today one who watches with solicitude both the things of God and the things of man, the needs of the spirit and the needs of the flesh, sees the return to these related but seemingly opposite heresies, the names of which our generation forgets but the ideas of which are still at work in our minds and hearts. Gnosticism and Manicheism are still alive, aggressive, unrestrained. Sometimes they are offered as a *new morality*—though they are centuries old, as old as the oldest temptations of our race, temptations both to presumption and to despair, to pride of flesh and to the foment of self-contempt.

But the Church still speaks with sanity of the supremacy, the dignity, the beauty of the flesh when it conforms to the plan, the loving law of its Creator and the grace of its Redeemer.

Undoubtedly, the Spirit of God "bloweth where He wills", and He comes to us not only through the spirits of men but also through the medium of the flesh and through the fleshly symbols which are the material of our daily lives as well as the instruments of His body— note well the word—which is the organized, institutional Church, the Church of the incarnate Word.

Specifically, on the level of human love made divine by a special sacrament, matrimony, under the guidance of our Holy Father Pope Paul and the teaching of the Vatican Council concerning the true nature, dignity, and sanctity of nuptial love, there is a growing awareness among Catholics that love must not be divorced from the primary purpose of marriage, which is the child, that love is really fruitful in the child, that the marriage debt must be regarded as an expression of love, not merely a demand of justice. Experience has proved that where the primary and secondary values of marriage are separated, there is danger that a man will take a wife for child-bearing and a mistress for lovemaking or, what has actually come to pass in much of our own society as a result of improved methods of birth prevention and easy divorce, turn his wife into a mistress until her ability to satisfy his lust wanes. Theologians of an earlier day were correct in censuring a love that sought expression in lust, for lust is a promiscuous tendency that must destroy love.

If it be true—thus far, God knows, it remains to be proved—that underneath the modern neopagan cult of the flesh there is the beginning of a new and sane humanism recognizing the dignity of the flesh and the full and true dignity of human nature, then, if this be true, there is needed more than ever a cult of Mary and of the virtues of which the Virgin is at once symbol, the realization by the power of God, and the example to us, her brothers and sisters.

There is needed more than ever a certain clear, powerful, persuasive witness, so long traditional in Christian spirituality. Sometimes it was made weak by neglect, by imperfect motives, by half-hearted practice, by obscure or negative understanding. But it produced not only saints but also civilization. It was the ancient Christian witness to such virtues and practices as chastity, virginity, celibacy, renunciation for the sake of the kingdom.

Thus by the teachings of the faith on the Madonna, the flesh is made the twin of the Spirit—no longer its rival, but one with the Spirit in love and service. Thus we become what man was when he walked in the garden, master of himself, steward (guardian) of all creation, the friend of God.

XIII

Mary the New Eve

It is a holy privilege and a most pleasant assignment
to speak of the grateful love—which is the essence of
piety—toward the Blessed Mother of God and the relationship of such piety to the Christian faith, which is the
essence of revealed religion, here in a corner of the world
where the Christian East and the Christian West meet.
Here the spiritual traditions of Orthodox Christianity,
culturally rich and multiple, coexist, with increasing
intimacy and mutuality, with the most loyal of attach-
ments of Catholicism, apostolic and Roman.

We find ourselves in a part of the world where both
those committed to Eastern Orthodoxy, present for the
most part in the West as in a diaspora but powerful and
enduring in the religious life of the East, and those
committed to Roman Catholicism, always present in the
East but in recent centuries chiefly dominant in the West,
have endured sufferings unto martyrdom because of
their respective and, in great measure, shared uncom-
promising faith in Jesus Christ. Their piety toward
Christ identified them as Christians, and their love for
His Blessed Mother, *Theotokos*, intensifies that identity
as Christians, complete Christians because of the manner
in which they find Christ, their Redeemer, really present
in the Eucharist, clearly speaking in the teaching Church,
mystically reproduced in their lives which relive all

This sermon was preached in Zagreb, Yugoslavia, on August 18,
1971, during the 13th International Marian Congress.

128

the mysteries of His life, His Passion, His death, His Resurrection, and His triumphant (let us not be ashamed of the word) victory over death, over error, and over every evil.

Because they are Christians, these Catholic and Orthodox faithful, they are brothers and sisters of Jesus Christ. Because of their unity in baptism and so rich communion in faith, they have the duty, not merely the privilege, of a certain fraternal correction, as indeed do all Christians, when they see one another in danger of wandering from the faith. An Orthodox prelate in my own country recently exercised this duty, to the joy of Catholics, when he corrected, on a national television program, a Catholic participant who had so far forgotten the ancient understanding of the liturgy that we Catholics and Orthodox share that he merited the rebuke (*mise au point*) publicly made in defense of the Catholic faith against a Catholic by the Orthodox metropolitan. So, too, a group of Orthodox theologians warned Catholics in America last October against the erroneous humanism which seems to be gathering momentum among some theologians, or, as they prefer to call themselves, *professional theologians*, in the Catholic community. They named specific *professional theologians* who, in the judgment of their Orthodox Christian critics, appear to have lost all *consciousness of identity* with what is known as the Church of the Apostles, Fathers, martyrs, and confessors. They expressed the fear that this disorientation in theology and the fast spread of secular theology by these and like theologians would reduce steadily the chances for Christian reunion.

One cannot deny the fraternal correction by these Orthodox brethren; in fact, an authentic Catholic would be grateful for it. However, one must make a single correction: The Orthodox critics of those *professional theologians* who play fast and loose with the faith referred to them as *Roman theologians*. They are, of course, nothing of the sort, as they would be the first to insist. The Orthodox Churches, as all know, have their own problem with *professional theologians* who, in spreading errors, do not speak for the Orthodox tradition. Our particular free-lancers of Catholic faith would resent nothing more violently than the accusation that they hold Roman positions in their theological speculations or that they are *Roman theologians*. We owe it to our Orthodox brethren to assure them that such is not the case—and, in so doing, we in no way offend the sensibilities of those who still claim the name of *Catholic* although they studiously reject the name of *Roman*.

Our Orthodox Christian brethren are perfectly aware that authentic Catholics see the Bishop of Rome as the bond of their unity, the *heart of hearts* in the visible Catholic Church. Catholics, as our Protestant brother, Roger Schutz, underlined at Fribourg last month, see in the Roman Pontiff the Universal Shepherd and in the Roman Church the Presidency of Charity.[1] Orthodox and Protestant Christians may interpret these dogmas in different ways, but they are properly scandalized, though not deceived, when *professional theologians*, calling themselves Catholics, try to explain away or diminish this central truth of the Roman Catholic creed: that as Christ is the invisible head of the Church, the successor of Peter is the visible head of the Church; that as the Church embraces by intent all the world, its center, for Catholics, is Rome; that no ecumenical spirit, however profound, prayerful, and insurgent can obscure the fact that the successor of Peter is the Vicar of Christ with all the teaching and directive plenitude of power that this truth implies. Authentic Protestants and faithful Orthodox understand this perfectly as the Catholic position, nor does it diminish their ecumenical spirit; only defective Catholics find fault with it.

Because the baptized Christians are brethren of Christ, they are children of Mary. There is nothing particularly mysterious about this; in fact, nothing could be more clear. How can we have Christ for our elder brother and not have piety toward Mary as Our Mother? Catholic and Orthodox Christians have always understood this. How can we truly perceive our relationship to Christ, the source of our redemption and, in the terms of Saint Paul in the first century and of Jacques Maritain in the present century, the very Person of the Church (the Church through which we are saved) unless we also acknowledge the privileges of Mary, the spotless Mother of Christ, the Mother of the Church and, therefore, the Mother of the Redeemed? She is, in Cardinal Newman's so profound phrase, the new Eve, mother of our supernatural lives, cause of our joy, even as the first Eve was the mother of our natural life and the source of our sorrow, the haunting sense of the collective guilt in the family, even in those who deny the fact of sin and certainly deny or define out of existence the sin of our first parents.

One cannot speak of the privileges of Mary as Mother of God without still bewildering in varying degrees even our most loving Protestant Christian brethren. But here in Zagreb, where Christian East and West meet as in few other places, where Catholics and Orthodox, despite any and all respective memories of even mutual resentment, nonetheless still rejoice together in the triumph of Christ, the majesty of God, and the memories of

Mother of God, we can and must speak of the manner in which the doctrines and cult surrounding the Blessed Mother intensify that Christian unity and piety made possible by, with, and in Christ.

The doctrine of Mary as *Theotokos* and devotion to the Virgin under this sublime title have always been bonds between East and West, as the Greek word reminds us. This doctrine of the divine maternity, the mystery that the Mother of Christ is the Mother of God, is veiled in wonder and eludes our human understanding. But it does so only because it is bound up with other mysteries no less shrouded in the same wonder and elusive for the same reasons, above all the mystery, unmistakably true but beyond our power to tell, that Mary's Son is at once true God and true man. Saint Cyril's account of why Mary is properly called *Theotokos* summarizes the teaching East and West have steadfastly shared:

> Therefore the Word indeed was God, but He became also man; and because He was born according to the flesh, because of His humanity, it is necessary that she who gave birth to Him should be the Mother of God. For if she did not give birth to God, certainly neither will He be called God Who was begotten of her. But if the divine Scriptures call Him God, she then gave birth to God made man because a man could not otherwise come to be except through generation from a woman. How then is not she who bore Him the Mother of God? That He is true God Who was born of her, we learn from the divine Scripture.

But there is a further understanding concerning the Blessed Mother which East and West should explore together and which provides further strong grounds ⸱r our common cult and increased unity: We must ⸱⸱erstand Mary's spiritual maternity. As mother of

Christ, Mary is somehow also mother of mankind. If by begetting Christ and bringing Him into the world Mary became the mother of God, so by the same maternity she became not only the mother of the Redeemer but the mother of the redeemed. Her maternity links her through Christ to God but also through Christ to us. Here, too, the place of Mary in the total economy of salvation is given focus, and the nature of the privileged relations between the devout and Divinity are clarified. By grace we are the children of God, the brethren of Jesus. In the mystery of that grace we are assimilated to Christ in a supernatural life which gives us a supernatural relationship to Mary and gives her a relationship to us. The mother of my Redeemer is somehow my mother, too. Saint Stanislas Kostka loved to repeat a claim consistent with the strictest theological accuracy and comprehensible to every Catholic and Orthodox mind and heart: "The Mother of God is my mother."

Here, too, is mystery profound and ineffable, but the mystery, again, surrounds *how* these wonders can be, not *whether* and *what* they are. When we speak of the spiritual maternity of Mary, of the Mother of Christ as the mother of all the redeemed, we speak a mystery, but we are not without insights to help us understand the mystery. These insights, we pray, will be studied together by Orthodox and Catholic theologians so that all who adore Christ and venerate His Mother may be brought closer to one another because of their understanding of something, at least, of what we mean by the marvelous titles that Eastern and Western Christians have not hesitated to give the Blessed Virgin, all of which derive from the central, supreme fact that she is the Mother of Christ.

Reflections on the Blessed Mother and on the unity w

have with her and with one another in, through, and because of Christ will nourish the desire for unity and will link that desire to its necessary dogmatic basis. For our human nostalgia for unity stems from the solidarity that once mankind had in Adam, while our divinely implanted desire for supernatural unity with one another and with God comes from the grace merited for us by Him through Whom and in Whom our reunion can alone be achieved, the new Adam Who is Christ Jesus.

The relation of the spiritual maternity of Mary to all these mysteries is suggested by Pope Benedict XV when he hails Mary as the new Eve, the spiritual mother of redeemed mankind, as Eve was the physical mother of our race.

> For as the first Adam had a woman as his associate in the Fall, so the second Adam willed that there participate in the reparation of our salvation she whom, by styling her "Woman" from the Cross, He declared to be the second Eve, that is, the ineffable sorrowing mother of all men, for whom He was dying, to win life for them.

God grant that, as we become more conscious of whose children we are, we may more joyfully recognize one another as brethren. For we are no longer merely the creatures of God but His sons and daughters, the brothers and sisters of His incarnate Son. "To as many as received Him, He gave the power to become the sons of God; for they are born, not of blood nor of the will of flesh nor of the will of man, but of God."[2] So we, one in Christ, are spiritually and supernaturally brethren in a family, the intimacy of which the world of sense and mere secular history cannot even guess. We are no longer Easterners or Westerners, save only in cherished secondary traditions, but are one people of God, thanks to the redemptive action of the new Adam and our ties in grace with the new Eve.

I have mentioned that Cardinal Newman has been, in the modern Church, the great theologian and preacher of Mary, Mother of Christ and Mother of the Church, as the new Eve. Cardinal Newman, one of the most persuasive and certainly the most clear of the theologians writing on the development of doctrine, would have had scant admiration for the demythologizers of Sacred Scripture. Though speculating, studying, and writing in the nineteenth century, he was completely at one with the great Fathers of the ancient Church in their so-close adherence to the very words, *ipsissima verba*, as well as the images and the witness, not merely the *spirit* or presumed secret sense, of Scripture. And so, with a literalness of understanding and a fidelity not only to the word of Scripture but to the interpretations of the Fathers, both of which would either scandalize or amuse many of our contemporary demythologizers of Sacred Scripture and the Christian message, Cardinal Newman asked this basic, comprehensive question: What is the great rudimental teaching of antiquity, from its earliest date, concerning Our Lady, the *prima facie* view of her person and place in the divine economy under which she comes to us in the writings of the Fathers of the Church?

He answers his own question in summary fashion: She is the second Eve. All the Mariology of Cardinal Newman—it is the Mariology of the Second Vatican Council in our own day and of the tradition of the Fathers of the East and the West through all these centuries—stems from this fact, a fact which Newman proclaims without apology, ambiguity, equivocal exegesis, or elaborate and erudite evasion.

It is refreshing, exciting, exhilarating, in these

when the bright stars of the Christian faith are obscured by so much theological smog, to read the unequivocal language in which Newman sets forth, as one of the greatest prelates in the world of modern theology, the childlike simplicity of the faith he shares with the Fathers of the Greek and the Latin Church.

Permit me to quote him:

[Mary] is the second Eve. Now let us consider what this implies. Eve had a definite, essential position in the First Covenant. The fate of the human race lay with Adam; he it was who represented us. It was in Adam that we fell; though Eve had fallen, still, if Adam had stood, we should not have lost those supernatural privileges which were bestowed upon him as our first father. Yet, though Eve was not the head of the race, still, even as regards the race, she had a place of her own; for Adam, to whom was divinely committed the naming of all things, named her "the mother of all the living", a name surely expressive not of a fact only but of a dignity; but further, as she thus had her own general relation to the human race, so again she had her own special place as regards its trial and its fall in Adam. In those primeval events, Eve had an integral share. "The woman, being seduced, was in the transgression." She listened to the evil angel; she offered the fruit to her husband, and he ate it. She cooperated, not as an irresponsible instrument, but intimately and personally in the sin: She brought it about. As the history stands, she was a *sine qua non*, a positive, active cause of it. And she had her share in its punishment; in the sentence pronounced on her, she was recognized as a real agent in the temptation and its issue, and she suffered accordingly. In that awful transaction there were three parties concerned—the serpent, the woman, and the man; nd at the time of their sentence, an event was announced for a distant future in which the three same parties were to meet again, the serpent, the woman, and the man; but it was to be a second Adam and a second Eve, and the new Eve was to be the mother of the new Adam: "I will put enmity between thee and the woman and between thy seed and her seed." The Seed of the Woman is the Word Incarnate, and the Woman, whose Seed or Son He is, is His Mother Mary. This interpretation and the parallelism it involves seem to me undeniable; but at all events (and this is my point) the parallelism is the doctrine of the Fathers, from the earliest times; and this being established, we are able, by the position and office of Eve in our fall, to determine the position and office of Mary in our restoration.

I shall adduce passages from the writings [of the Fathers], noting their respective countries and dates; and the dates shall extend from their births or conversions to their deaths, since what they propound is at once the doctrine which they had received from the generation before them and doctrine which was accepted and recognized as true by the generation to whom they transmitted it.[3]

The great convert-Cardinal then lists and quotes from Fathers of the Church from every corner of Christendom, notably Saint Justin, Saint Irenaeus, and Tertullian. He summarized their witness by saying:

Now, what is especially noticeable in these three writers is that they do not speak of the Blessed Virgin merely as the physical instrument of Our Lord's taking flesh but as an intelligent, responsible cause of it; her faith and obedience being the accessories to the Incarnation and gaining it as her reward. As Eve failed in these virtues, and thereby brought on the fall of the race in Adam, so Mary by means of the same had a part in its restoration. . . .

137

However, not to go beyond the doctrine of the three Fathers, they unanimously declare that she was not a mere instrument in the Incarnation, such as David or Judah may be considered; they declare she cooperated in our salvation not merely by the descent of the Holy Ghost upon her body but by specific holy acts, the effect of the Holy Ghost within her soul; that, as Eve forfeited privileges by sin, so Mary earned privileges by the fruits of grace; that, as Eve was disobedient and unbelieving, so Mary was obedient and believing; that, as Eve was a cause of ruin to all, Mary was a cause of salvation to all; that, as Eve made room for Adam's fall, so Mary made room for Our Lord's reparation of it; and thus, whereas the free gift was not as the offence, but much greater, it follows that, as Eve cooperated in effecting a great evil, Mary cooperated in effecting a much greater good.

And besides the run of the argument, which reminds the reader of Saint Paul's antithetical sentences in tracing the analogy between Adam's work and Our Lord's work, it is well to observe the particular words under which the Blessed Virgin's office is described. Tertullian says that Mary "blotted out" Eve's fault and "brought back the female sex" of "the human race to salvation", and Saint Irenaeus says that "by obedience was she the cause or occasion [whatever was the original Greek word] of salvation to herself and the whole human race"; that by her the human race is saved; that by her Eve's complication is disentangled; and that she is Eve's advocate, or friend in need.[4]

Whereupon Cardinal Newman, always enamored of the Fathers and the great Tradition, as are all authentic Catholics and faithful Orthodox, invokes a veritable litany of Fathers of the East and of the West in support of his concept of the new Eve which is, in the final analysis, the basic premise and first principle of that special relationship to the redeemed, the people of God, the living Church, all of which is summed up in the title Mother of God as also Mother of the Church. Of the numerous Fathers of the Church invoked by Newman in the same sense, but in varying terms, none is more eloquent or clear than Saint Epiphanius. His words, as quoted by Cardinal Newman, constitute a summary and synthesis of the shared faith of Catholics and Orthodox concerning Mary, the basis of their piety toward her, the ground of our ecumenical hopes that the Church, which has broken down all walls of division between us, may be ever more manifestly the bond of our unity. Saint Epiphanius holds forth the promise of a Christian unity of *living faith, unconquerable hope, flaming charity—the unity of those who live by one sole life, the life of God Himself that comes to us through Christ, Who became incarnate among us by the power of the Holy Spirit when He was born of Mary.*

The words of Saint Epiphanius, which meant so much to Newman and mean so much to us in Zagreb, are words which no human respect, no academic confusion or theological fog may prevent us from transmitting to those who will come after us in the Church and whose Christian piety must necessarily include piety toward the Blessed Mother.

He said:

It is she [Mary] whom Eve represents—Eve who, strangely, was named "mother of all the living". . . . And the wonder was that after the Fall she received this title. So far as the body is concerned, Eve was certainly the mother of every man on earth; but from Mary the Life itself was born in the world, so that she could bear living things and become their mother. And so, curiously, she too, is called "Mother of all the living". . . . But there is another marvel about these two which must be considered; Eve became the cause of man's death . . . but Mary the cause of his life . . . so that life might be born in place of death, life eliminating the death which came from the woman. The Life is none other than He Who, through the Woman, has become our life.[5]

If, then, piety is the virtue which binds us to the sources of all life, to God, to our parents, to the Church, to Christ, certainly Christian piety binds us, in grateful love, to Mary—or our acceptance of Christ and of the mystery of our kinship with Him is imperfect, partial, and unfulfilled.

XIV

Mary, Type of Servant
And Agent of the Holy Spirit

The Blessed Virgin Mary is the Mother of the Church and therefore the example, as well as the guide and inspiration, of everyone who, in and through the Church, seeks to be the servant of God and man and the obedient agent of the promptings of the Holy Spirit.

The Holy Spirit, as Pope Leo XIII reminded us, is the soul of the Church: All the activity and service of the members of the Church, beginning with the supreme participation of the Blessed Mother in the work of the Church, is vivified by the Holy Spirit as the body, in all its activities, is vivified by its soul. The Holy Spirit is the Paraclete, Advocate, and Comforter which Christ Himself sent to be our consolation in the sorrowful mysteries of life, our source of moderation in the joyful mysteries of life, our added principle of exaltation in the glorious mysteries of life.

So He was for the Blessed Mother; so also He is for the least of us; so also He is for the rest of the Church, even for those who are its *unconscious* but *conscientious* members.

Wherever there is *faith* there is the example of Mary, because she lived by faith as the Scriptures remind us so many times: at Bethlehem, in Nazareth, in Egypt, seeking the Child in the Temple, at Cana, as she listened to Jesus preach, herself lost in the crowd, in anguish on

This paper was delivered at the Pontificium Athenaeum Antonianum, Rome, Italy, on May 19, 1975.

the way to Calvary, at the foot of the Cross, and finally in the Cenacle. Wherever there is *hope* it is in imitation of Mary, sustained by the Spirit to which she had been obedient as all of us who hope obey, quietly and patiently, the indwelling Spirit. Wherever there is *love* or charity diffused in the hearts of the faithful, in Saint Paul's phrase, there is the result of the loving obedience by which Mary brought among us Charity Incarnate and thus became the Mother of the Church of which her Son was the founder and remains the invisible head.

Clearly then, there is no obedience or devotion to the Holy Spirit, the Paraclete sent by Jesus, apart from Christ Who sent Him and the Incarnation to which Mary gave the flesh of our human nature. There may be legitimate theological debate about the precise sense in which we have access to Christ and to His saving grace through Mary: *per Mariam ad Christum*. There may be speculation on the theological and spiritual meaning of this axiom, but no informed Catholic will be confused by that speculation or in doubt about the basic meaning of that phrase. There may be an element of obscurity in the minds of some who fail to perceive the intimate relationship between Christ and His Church and the necessity of the mediation of the Church between the believer and the Redeemer, but such obscurity will be limited to those preoccupied with institutional concepts or structural problems rather than sensitive to the fact that the Holy Catholic Church is at once *organized* and *organic*, organized by Christ and vivified by the Holy Spirit, again the soul of the Church. Most understand perfectly the cry of Saint Joan: "Why do you make it so difficult? I make no difference between Christ and His Church! It is all one!"

There may be those who cherish the illusion of direct access by humanity to the Holy Spirit of God, forgetting the whole of salvation history and bypassing the fact of the Incarnation and the relationship of that Incarnation in its every *fleshy* and human implication in favor of a *mysticism* which, whatever it may be, is not Christian and certainly not Catholic. The Incarnation and the consequent living presence of Christ in His Church, along with the place of the Church in the scheme of salvation, include at every point and at every level the operation of the Holy Spirit—and so any mystical cult that makes theological sense, since the day when the power of the Most High overshadowed Mary so that she through faith gave human flesh to the Eternal Son of God and since the day when the incarnate Son of God sent the Paraclete that our faith in Christ and identification with the Church might be clarified and reinforced, since those times all possible Catholic devotion to the Holy Spirit has been necessarily *incarnational*, in no way bypassing the Body and Blood of Christ, the incarnate Person of Christ, the historical reality of His Church or the example of Mary Immaculate as the type of all authentic service and cult of the Holy Spirit.

It becomes, then, transparently clear that devotion to the Holy Spirit and the perpetuation of the graces and charisms poured forth on the first Pentecost or later involve no species of *elitism*: It is the common calling of all those of whom the Church is the Mother and Mary is the example.

It is good to fix our attention on the Blessed Virgin Mary as the type of the servant and agent of the Holy Spirit in these days when the Incarnation appears t strike some as too *earthy*, too *fleshy*, too *physical*. Such outlook sees the Church as too much a part of the history of this world and Mary as too *sentimental* and *pietistic* for the devotion of the elitist who, in enthusiastic fashion, seeks a direct access to the purely spiritual God. He is impatient with the concepts of the Incarnation and the Church which include elements so close to flesh and blood as the sacraments and the Sacred Heart of the Nazarene Who was the Eternal Son of God and the descendant, according to the flesh, of David as well as a litany of sinners recorded in the genealogies of Jesus in the Gospels, although, of course, through the privileges of Mary His Mother, the immediate human nature of which He was born was totally free from sin but still flesh, Jewish, and bound by the space and time of the creation brought to pass by God the Father, the First Person of the adorable Trinity.

The most superficial reading of the Sacred Scriptures reveals that in the mighty work of the Incarnation, the central event of history and the blending of all of heaven and all of earth, there is a total absence of mystical fireworks from the words, actions, and spirit of Mary. There is spiritual exaltation, of course, in the hymn of praise to the God of Abraham which is the *Magnificat*. There is the anxiety, if you will, of a mother living by faith, not vision, as she seeks out and seems to rebuke her Son lost to the caravan but present in the Temple under circumstances obviously mysterious to her, in her solicitude yet faith at the marriage feast of Cana. In her, for the most part, silent participation in His redemptive life and Passion, from the apparition of the angel to the Cenacle, the descent of the Holy Spirit, and her quiet entrance into the care of Saint John of which we know so little, there is eloquent silence, a mood of meditation and storing up

144

of mysteries in her heart which reflect her determination in faith and love to obey the precept of the Old Testament: "Be still and know that I am God."[1]

In her special relation to the Holy Spirit her phrase, typical of the servant and agent of that Spirit, is brief, dramatic, obedient, and self-effacing, though that phrase is the turning point of salvation history: It is the phrase by which all of heaven and earth blossomed in beauty at a Baby's birth as the renewal of the world became possible, as through Christ the Church became a reality, and as the kingdom of God on earth became a hope for sinful mankind: "Behold the handmaid of the Lord; be it done to me according to thy word."[2]

Thus Mary corresponded with the power of the Most High and by the overshadowing power of the Holy Spirit became the perfect type of that Spirit's servant and agent. It is the universal spirit expressed in these words which has at all times constituted the essence of authentic Catholic Christian spirituality. It has always been identified as *openness to the Holy Spirit*. Alas, it may in some times and places have been neglected, as have been all virtues, usually as a consequence of lack of *openness to the Holy Spirit*—but it has been the explanation of all the sanctity in every nation and every place of which Mary has been the exemplar as Queen of the Saints and in which the Church has been the source as custodian, in a sense well understood by the faithful, of the sacramental and doctrinal treasures left us by Christ and protected across the ages by the Paraclete.

A contemporary poet has perhaps come closest to expressing this *openness to the Spirit* when, almost in a paraphrase of Mary's "Behold the handmaid of the Lord", he has urged us always to say Yes to God, never say No to the promptings of His Spirit, the commandments of His Son, the guidance of His Church. Mary's Yes to God was flaming with meaning; it was an unqualified assent, without reserve and without either false humility or futile dramatics. It was given in that holy silence in which, being still, we discover the existence and reality of God. No form of Christian spirituality which lacks these characteristics can be seen as the imitation of Mary, the perfect type of the servant and agent of the Holy Spirit.

Mary walked, as we have said, by faith, not vision, real or pretended. She knew fear; she suffered from limited understanding and every human misgiving consistent with her sinless nature. She was what each of us must be if we are truly servants and agents of the Holy Spirit. It is in her constant Yes to God's will and to the promptings of the Holy Spirit that we are called to imitate her, not with holy histrionics, but with the silence that reigned as the angels softly sang at Bethlehem and in the entire life of Mary from the valley of Nazareth to the hill of Calvary.

It is amazing how, even when we combine her words in the public revelations of Scripture to those attributed to her in private revelations throughout history, we find them to be so *few*. They would hardly constitute a brief homily. Surely there is a lesson in this for all of us who wish to be the servants and agents of the Holy Spirit in the pattern of Mary. It is significant that silence and patience always surround the *Fiat*, the Yes to God, when whatever angel or other channel of God's message brings us the promptings of the Holy Spirit.

"Dum medium silentium tenerent omnia, et nox in ịo cursu medium iter haberet. . . ." For while all

146

things were in quiet silence and the night was in the midst of her course, Thy Almighty Word leapt down from Thy royal throne.[3] True, He did so as a result of Mary's *Fiat*, her Yes to the Holy Spirit, and came in order that the Spirit of the Lord [might be] upon Him "to preach the gospel to the poor, to heal the contrite of heart, to preach deliverance to the captives, . . . and set at liberty them that are bruised."[4] But let us note carefully how it all began with silence. Only in such silence can we expect the recurrence of the coming together of shepherds and kings, while angels sing and the tumult grows prayerfully but dynamically silent.

Next to docility and closely related to it, the greatest gift of the Holy Spirit to Mary seems to have been *patience*. From her we other clients of the Holy Spirit, brethren of Christ, children of God, learn best how to live the word of Scripture: "In patientia vestra possidebitis animas vestras." In your patience you shall possess your souls.[5]

Of all her examples to us of how we should be the servants of the Holy Spirit, this is Mary's most timely and opportune lesson in this age of aimless activism, spiritual restlessness, noisy, agitated, and polarized religiosity. *Pax nobis! Shalom! Be still—and know that I am God!*[6]

Appendix

Some Street Shrines of Rome

I

As the Holy Year pilgrim wends his way through the streets of Rome, he will be continually impressed by the great number of sacred images erected for popular veneration on the walls of public and private buildings, at corners and crossings, as well as under archways.

Most of these street shrines—they number hundreds —pay Roman homage to the Blessed Mother of God and are known by the Roman people as the *madonnelle*. They bear eloquent, enduring witness to the love of the Queen City of Christendom for the Queen of all the saints.

The piety of Rome has found this typical expression from earliest Christian antiquity, and the perennial vitality of the tradition is revealed by the manner in which each succeeding century has replaced with its own characteristic shrines the monuments of the epoch before. In the process of rebuilding by which the face of Rome is continually renewed, all but a precious few of the oldest shrines have disappeared. Some still survive from the fifteenth century, but most of the shrines which grace the streets of Rome today belong to the sixteenth through the eighteenth centuries.

Variations in style and artistic merit are many and sharp, but all the street shrines—the rude, colorful, and

This article was written for and published in the January 1950 issue of the *American Ecclesiastical Review*.

naive *madonnelle* of the back streets or the poor quarters and the resplendent baroque Madonnas, Roman in their elegance and impressive in their quality—all have one purpose: the praise of Mary, *Regina Romanorum*.

The appeal to piety of some of these outdoor chapels is most powerful. Often surrounded by many *ex-voto* and fragrant with flowers freshly placed before them, they serve as oases of holy calm in the midst of the turbulence of everyday life. A comforting light frequently shines from them, and the passerby, lifting his eyes to images discolored by time and elements, feels his mind and heart lifted for a moment above human affairs; his worries of the hour are quieted by these omnipresent mementos of heaven and of things eternal.

Several of the most ancient street images became so greatly venerated among the people for the marvels associated with them that they were removed to nearby churches for more worthy enshrinement and more regular cult.

Beneath one of the arches of the famous Theatre of Pompei, opposite the archway of the Cenci, there used to be a fourteenth-century image of the Mother and Child painted by an unknown artist. On January 10, 1546, two men came to blows before it. One was about to strike his opponent with a lethal weapon when the other cried out, "For love of Our Lady, don't kill me!" At these words the assailant checked himself and letting his weapon fall, embraced his intended victim. The latter, thus mercifully spared, straightway fell on his erstwhile adversary and savagely murdered him. At this horrifying scene tears rushed from the eyes of the Madonna. The extraordinary event brought together citizens from every part of Rome, and so great was the reverence thenceforth shown the image that it was necessary to remove it from the wall and place it over the main altar of a chapel dedicated to S. Salvatore in Cacabariis, where it was splendidly adorned by a Florentine nobleman, Nicola Acciajuoli. The miracles worked there by God, through the intercession of His Holy Mother, increased both faith and fervor, and the chapel in time was built into a church completed in 1612 under the patronage of S. Maria del Pianto. The image was crowned by the Vatican Chapter, May 20, 1643.

The *Madonna della Lettera*, painted in 1654 by Nicolo Pomancio in a recess of the wall at the foot of the stairs leading to St. Peter in Montorio, was credited with the instant cure of a nun dying in the nearby Monastery of the Seven Sorrows. The sister had been anointed with oil from a lamp burning before the sacred image. Because of the immense popularity of the shrine, Clement XI had the image removed from the wall on August 9, 1714, and transported with great solemnity into the church of St. Peter in Montorio, where it is still venerated. In recognition of the miracles associated with it, the image was crowned by the Vatican Chapter in 1717.

A blind man, finding himself on the ground floor of a humble house near the church of S. Salvatore della Corte in Trastevere, suddenly heard the noise of falling stones. Seized with fear that he might be buried under what he thought was the ruins of the roof, he turned quickly to flee but was amazed to find himself able to see. The first object of his restored vision was an image of Mary with Child, surrounded by an extraordinary splendor. With cries of "Light! light!" the poor man invited everyone in the neighborhood to admire the sacred image which had been laid bare by the collapse of an old wall and which he swore, gave sight to him. The news of the wonder spread throughout the city. The first to rush to the scene were the blind and the crippled, begging to be healed of their infirmities. The flow of people into the humble place so increased that the cardinal vicar, by a decree on August 8, 1730, ordered the image removed to the church of S. Salvatore della Corte. The church became commonly called S. Maria della Luce from that day.

The *Madonna di Strada Cupa* was so called because it had been painted on the wall of a vineyard in a dark street of Trastevere. The news of the graces constantly received by the devotees of this shrine soon passed the limits of the section and spread throughout the city. People came from every side in pilgrimage of prayer and praise so that Urban VIII, after careful examination of the miracles, ordered the picture detached from the wall and transported into the basilica of S. Maria in Trastevere. The removal took place during the night of June 27, 1624, and the holy image, covered by a cloth, was temporarily placed in the cemetery adjoining the basilica until the end of the process required to authenticate two of the most impressive miracles: the restoration to life of a certain Giuseppe Sperandini and the instantaneous cure of a blind child. On the following July 21, at the completion of the process, the image was uncovered in the basilica for the veneration of the rejoicing people. This image, too, was crowned by the Vatican Chapter, April 5, 1634.

The *Madonna delle Grazie*, in the church of the Most Holy Trinity of the Pilgrims, is a fresco that was first on the wall of the Capranica Palace on Via della Valle. Because of the constant gatherings of the devout, Church thorities decided to remove it from the public thoroughfare and place it in a more convenient location. The Archconfraternity of Pilgrims asked to have responsibility for its care, and with the consent of the owners of the palace, it was taken into their church on July 8, 1562. After many cures had been attributed to the shrine, the Vatican Chapter crowned it on June 21, 1654.

The *Madonna degli Angeli*, which had been painted on the wall of a street in Campo Marzio, had to be removed from the public highway because of the great numbers attracted by news of miracles. In order to solve the problem created for coachmen who wished to guide their carriages through the busy thoroughfare, the Association of Coachmen proposed to have the image moved into a church, and in 1545, with the permission of Paul III, they carried the miraculous image in solemn procession to the church of S. Lucia della Tinta, where the Association customarily met. There is a strong suggestion of precipitate action by the coachmen in the account of the transfer. A skilled mason detached the shrine from the wall. Brocades of silver and gold, torches, and whatever else was necessary for a splendid procession were prepared. Mortar and the needed implements were ready in front of the church of St. Lucy; the members of the Association in full regalia and the porters in prescribed frock were ready to put their shoulders to the sacred burden. But when they bent to their task, the image became immovable. Efforts were repeated to no avail. Those who were wise quickly understood and the chronicle tells us that a tardy invitation was straightway sent to the local clergy to join the procession! Then with the greatest ease the Madonna was carried to its place amidst a harmony of instruments and the glad cries of the people.

The *Madonna della Misericordia*, in the church of St. John dei Fiorentini, was at one time a fresco on a small street called *delle Palle*, near the church. As its name would indicate, it was a place where youngsters played ball. One day an impious contestant, in a rage at losing a game, turned on the sacred image and struck it with his ball, leaving a livid mark on the cheek under the right eye. Even today one may perceive the traces of the alleged blow. The crime had been public and so, the tradition asserts, publicly and instantly the criminal was punished by the paralysis of his arm. Contrite and tearful, the wretched man asked the *Madre della Misericordia* her forgiveness; the cure of his arm followed forty days later. The image was immediately acclaimed by the residents of the neighborhood, among whom Florentines were prominent. They asked permission to transport the image to their church, and the miraculous image was placed in a chapel adjoining the main altar, decorated with the gilded plaster works and paintings of the era. On March 22, 1648, at the request of the Florentine nobles, the image was crowned by the Vatican Chapter.

On the outer wall of a dwelling on Via Parione as late as 1535 there was a painting of an image of Mary with the Divine Child. It was located near a well and had been greatly venerated in the crowded neighborhood. One day, so runs the legend, a gambler, in a fit of anger and cursing obscenely, threw a stone at the image. Immediately the face of Mary was stained with apparent blood, traces of which still remain on one eyebrow and on the throat. Bystanders were stupefied, then ran to wipe the miraculous liquid with linen cloths; others turned on the impious offender and delivered him to the police. The object of the sacrilege was detached from the

154

wall and taken to the nearby parochial church of St. Mary and St. Gregory in Vallicella. In 1575, in the days of St. Philip Neri, the little church was transformed into the present sumptuous temple commonly called the *Chiesa Nuova*. The image was crowned by the Vatican Chapter on July 9, 1649.[1]

The image of *S. Maria in Posterula* was once located on the house where the pastor of S. Biagio della Tinta lived. In 1573 a blind man begged Mary for the grace of sight. One day while he was praying he suddenly opened his eyes and saw the image. Neighbors, startled by his cries, came in such crowds that it was considered best to remove the shrine from above the pastor's door and place it in the church.

The *Madonna dell'Orazione* in the Chiesa della Morte had once been a painting on the outer wall of a stable. The Confraternity of the Company of the Dead asked the owner if they might keep it in their church because of the great veneration in which it was held. Permission was granted, and in 1577 they installed it with great solemnity on the main altar. On November 6, 1661, the Vatican Chapter proceeded with the coronation of the image in recognition of its miracles.

The *Madonna della Salute* had also been a painting on a street in the Borgo. In 1659 the Chierici Regolari delle Scuole Pie had it removed from the wall and taken to the church of St. Lawrence in the Borgo. It was called *Madonna della Salute* because of the many cures it had effected and was crowned by the Vatican Chapter December 6, 1696.

In 1426 the Ardicini cardinals commissioned a painting of Our Lady on the facade of their palace in the Borgo. The gracefulness of its design and the beauty of its col quickly drew the prayerful attention of passersby, and very soon the whole was covered with votive memorials. For greater reverence a railing like a choir screen was placed in front of it. In 1657 the heirs of the Ardicini gave the painting to the Confraternity of the Most Blessed Sacrament. The news of its miracles constantly spread, and the image was brought in solemn procession to the church of St. Joachim at Scosacavalli, where the Vatican Chapter crowned it in 1664.

Some of Rome's most celebrated churches were built to honor other images of Our Lady which first were venerated as popular shrines in the public streets.

For example, there was an image under the portico of the ancient church of St. Andrew of the Acquaricciari, in the Parione section, during the pontificate of Sixtus IV, a time in which Italy was made bloody by constant battles among the states. The Pontiff implored Our Lady to restore peace among his people, promising to erect a church to house the Madonna of the portico in Parione. Such a church did in fact arise in thanksgiving for the grace obtained, the magnificent *S. Maria della Pace*.

Under Pope Alexander VI, several prosperous merchants cooperated with twelve associations of workmen to erect the church of *S. Maria dell'Orto* to safeguard a Madonna painted above a garden gate in Trastevere. It had miraculously cured the owner from the last stages of an incurable disease. Following numerous miracles, this image, too, was crowned by the Vatican Chapter on August 19, 1657.

The church of *S. Maria della Scala* was built by the Cardinal Tolomeo Gallio da Como with the offerings of lovers of Mary who particularly admired a picture painted under the outer stairway of a small house in

Trastevere. In 1592 it had reportedly healed a deaf-mute child. The church was completed by the nephew of Cardinal Tolomeo, who transported the image there after it had been detached from the wall. In 1597 Clement VIII gave the church to the Carmelites, who received for their Madonna the gold crown from the Vatican Chapter in 1646.

In 1681 the church of the *Madonna dei Miracoli* in the Piazza del Popolo was consecrated. It had been built to safeguard a miraculous image painted on cloth formerly venerated in a small church on the bank of the Tiber, near Porta Flaminia. This little church had been built in 1525 to honor a yet earlier image painted under an archway on the bank of the river, which had been invoked by a drowning child and had given to the chapel the name *Madonna dei Miracoli*. But in 1598 Cardinal Antonio Salviati wished to give the miraculous image to the church of St. Joachim of the Incurables which he had built, and so he caused a copy to be made on like cloth for the chapel, a copy to bear and to merit the title *dei Miracoli*.

S. Maria delle Fornaci was built to house a miraculous image of Mary which a priest, Giuseppe Faraldi, had commissioned from the Flemish painter Egidio Alet to be placed outside the Porta Cavalleggeri at a place where young men used to gather. The painting speedily became an object of popular cult, especially among the young, and in 1691 the present building was raised on the designs of Andrea Pozzo.

The *Madonna della Purità* was painted on the wall of the home of a certain Lucrezia Salviati in the Borgo. During the Sack of Rome in 1527 the Bourbon soldiers burned the house; debris covered the picture, and the plac became a rubbish dump. Later the retreating waters of a flood uncovered the picture of Mary. A woman with a crippled hand, passing by the spot, saw the face emerging from the ruins and, as if by inspiration, cried out in prayer and praise. Hardly had she spoken when she was perfectly cured. The miracle aroused such great interest that popular offerings made it possible to construct a church into which the image was transferred. The church, *S. Maria della Purità*, later fell into neglect, but the shrine is now in the oratory of S. Maria in Trasportina.

In 1668 the Abbot Farsetti, a Venetian nobleman, commissioned Gagliardi di Città di Castello to paint "a devout image of Mary nursing her Divine Child" for public veneration in a dingy alley existing at that time hard by the Palazzo Venezia. The priest's intention was to sanctify the place, which was considered dangerous. Eventually the end of the alley was transformed into an oratory which in 1677 was splendidly decorated through the generosity of Antonio Barbaro, Ambassador of the Republic of Venice. In 1682 the Marquis Francesco Ruspoli had an altar constructed of choice marble in thanksgiving for a miraculous healing he received through intercession before this image.

Perhaps the most widely renowned of the street shrines later translated into churches is the shrine of Our Lady of the Way. The *Madonna della Strada* takes us back to 425 when the Roman, Giulio Astalli, in the days of Pope Celestine I, erected a church in honor of the Virgin Mary in Section VIII of the ancient city. This shrine is sometimes called the *Madonna degli Astalli*. There are differences of opinion concerning the precise origins of its name, but it seems most likely that it was named *Madonna degli Astalli* because of a church erected by the

Astalli family and *Madonna della Strada* because it had first been on the wall of a public street.

When St. Ignatius Loyola was in Rome he celebrated Mass before this image every day, having obtained possession of the church from Pope Paul III for the order he had founded. In 1568 Cardinal Alessandro Farnese decided to provide for the growing cult and larger parish by erecting the imposing Church of the Gesù. The *Madonna della Strada* was placed in the rich chapel where it is still venerated, a chapel of splendid marbles and precious trophies testifying to the gratitude of the devout multitudes for the innumerable blessings received through Mary for the Roman people.

The devotional history of Rome includes many chapters centering about the street shrines. One of the most dramatic of these involves certain seemingly supernatural events which occurred in 1796 and which caused the Romans to turn even more fervently to their street shrines. Several images of the Blessed Virgin venerated in the public streets were reported to have moved their eyes miraculously. The city was thrown into a hubbub by the extraordinary events. The populace hurried in crowds to whatever places reported the marvels, giving rise to moving scenes of popular faith.

Some idea of the profound echo these incidents had in the souls of the Roman people may be gleaned from a few quotations from chronicles of the time.

> While Rome was envying the happy lot of the people of Ancona and the other cities of the Marches for having been worthy to witness great miracles worked by God by means of the sacred images of His Holy Mother with the opening, closing, and turning of her eyes, this capitol of the Catholic world in turn obtained a similar favor

On the morning of Saturday, July 9, the day especially dedicated to the glories of Mary, at about eleven o'clock several devout persons, religious among them, pausing to pray to Our Lady of the Archway, observed that the miraculous image was turning and raising its eyes. At such an extraordinary sight (*prodigio*) the people quickly assembled crowds so great that the authorities found it necessary to station soldiers to maintain order. The Blessed Virgin did not limit herself to working the wonder through this sacred image alone; soon after, the prodigy was repeated in the cases of many others located on various streets. On Sunday and Monday a number of prodigies occurred at other images venerated in churches, e.g., *S. Maria del Popolo*, *S. Maria in Vallicella*, *S. Marcello agli Agonizzanti*, and *S. Marcello agli Bonfratelli*, etc., where the faithful also reported receiving many graces.

It was also observed that on two dry branches of lilies, which had been attached to the wall under the *Madonna dell'Arco de' Pantani*—one more than a year before, the other several months before—four green buds appeared on Saturday, flourishing before the very eyes of the people.

On the occasion of these great marvels the Holy Father, in order to encourage his beloved people even more to penance and to sincere reconciliation with God, published through Cardinal della Somaglia, his vicar, a call to attendance at the missions which were to begin on Sunday the tenth at 9:30 in the evening in six designated squares: in Piazza Navona, preached by Benedetto Fenaja, a mission father; in Piazza Barberini, with Father Giovanni Marchetti; in Piazza Colonna, with Father Vincenzo da S. Paolo, a Passionist; in Piazza di S. Maria in Trastevere, with Father Giuseppe Marconi; in Piazza di S. Maria de' Monti, with Father Giuseppe Natale dal Pino; in Piazza di S. Giacomo in Borgo, with Father Guiseppe della Casa, a parish priest.

The crowds of people who gathered at these missions were filled with holy fervor. Not only did they move in throngs from one image of Mary to another reciting the rosary and the litanies but in the evenings, late into the night, numberless processions were seen—men, women, and children, persons of every quality and circumstance, and even the crippled—singing the praises of the Blessed Virgin. In her honor the city was illumined by the faithful so that it seemed like day, and the whole spectacle aroused the most tender and holy satisfaction. . . . On Wednesday the missions appointed for the profit of souls ended in the same six squares. His Eminence, Cardinal della Somaglia, seconding the pious wish of the Roman people themselves, thought it well to invite religious communities, confraternities, and all pious associations generally to satisfy their holy desires by well-ordered penitential processions conducted without pomp. These proceeded in prayer to their favorite churches. . . .

. . . On Thursday afternoon, the people gathered in Piazza Navona for a penitential procession. The crucifix was carried by a member of the Venerable Archconfraternity of the Sacconi and was followed by cardinals in purple vestments, a large number of priests also in vestments, and by many of the nobility. The people then followed in great numbers, in the best possible order and directed by their priests. After the men came a vast throng of women following a sacred image of Mary which was carried by the Princess Doria.

When the procession arrived at St. Peter's the crowd assembled in orderly fashion in the square which, though huge, was too small for their number. Father Fenaja ascended a rostrum and preached with zeal urging the people to increased devotion to Mary. Meanwhile Monsignor Brancadoro, Archbishop of Nisibi, vested and took the Blessed Sacrament from a special altar and carried it in procession to a magnificent altar erected at the head of the steps of the basilica, where basilica musicians sang the prescribed prayers and the prelate gave solemn Benediction. After this the procession dispersed, and the people left in groups, reciting the rosary and singing hymns of praise.

In the eyes of the chronicler the city seemed transformed: Our parents certainly never saw—nor, perhaps, will our children ever see—the city of Rome present such a spectacle as it presented in that memorable epoch. Everything focused on one central fact: Appearance, manners, speech; the streets, the squares, the stores, the houses, the churches showed changes which would seem incredible even to us who saw them. The holy names of Jesus and Mary were on all lips, as though they were the delight of all hearts. During the day one encountered at every step shrines where the Mother of God, who is also our Mother, was constantly entreated by devout throngs praying on their knees, seeking graces or joyfully and gratefully applauding the recurrence of the miracle. This one was full of remorse; that one beat his breast; another had eyes wet with tears. The sacred images of the loving Mother were no longer left abandoned during the long days and short nights of this warm season. At dusk each evening another tender spectacle might be observed as the faithful, no longer singly but now in groups of greater or lesser number, walked from their homes to the local shrines singing various praises in sweet harmony, alternating with the refrain repeated by all: *Evviva Maria, Evviva Gesù; Evviva Maria e Chi La Creò!*

At the last two missions the Pope himself, Pius VI, was present.

On Monday His Holiness went to the Piazza Barberini where he heard the mission preached by Abbot Marchetti from the balcony of a private house which had been fittingly decorated. At the end of the mission ceremony, he descended to a room prepared as a vestry and there vested. Preceded by the Papal Cross he passed to a nearby altar where the Most Blessed Sacrament taken from the church of the Capuchin Fathers was already exposed. After he had genuflected, assisted by the prelates of his private chamber, he gave Benediction to the vast crowd assembled in that huge square. The ceremony concluded, His Holiness unvested, and in the midst of the acclamations of the crowd he returned to his residence in the Quirinal. On Tuesday His Holiness came out again and went to the palace of the viceregent of the city where he listened from a beautifully decorated window to the mission preached by Father Vincenzo, the Passionist. At its conclusion he gave solemn Benediction to the crowd which filled the square. . . .

Even a year later the enthusiasm of the people had not died out. On July 9, 1797, a great feast of thanksgiving was celebrated in the churches of Rome in memory of the marvelous movement of the eyes which had taken place the year before and had occasioned the unprecedented missions and public devotions. Every image of Our Lady on the public streets of Rome was restored if necessary and in each case beautifully decorated for the solemn anniversary of the prodigies.

But if the street shrines were scenes of joyful and glorious mysteries, so also they were destined for sorrowful experiences. The memories of the miracles of the *madonnelle* were still fresh when Rome was occupied by the French troops. The Pope was exiled, the churches stripped and largely closed, the clergy were hounded, and religious observances were forbidden. In such a season it was inevitable that the shrines in the streets of Rome became frequent objects of vandalism. The chronicler records several sad incidents of sacrilege:

> . . . Last night the image which was on the corner of the Bonaccorsi Palace was prudently removed from its niche. Several other images were broken that same night with stone, for which reason many have already been removed in order not to expose them to similar insults. One of them, the *Madonna della Pietà*, located over the store of a merchant named Montanari on the street from Piazza Colonna to Montecitorio, was even pelted with excrement. In broad daylight stones were thrown at another image on the Corso, and orders were given to have it removed. Whoever would have believed such acts of impiety could be committed without punishment in Rome? . . .
>
> . . . During the past two nights other images have been smashed by stones, and for this reason they and others which had been spared were removed from their niches. Some of the people, however, especially in Borgo, in Trastevere, and in Monti, would not take down the shrines; others placed in the niches paper images as temporary substitutes and kept the lamps lit there at night as if the real ones were still there. . . . For several nights the people kept watch in order to trap the unruly stone throwers.

At long last the period of anarchy came to its end, and Rome triumphantly acclaimed the returning Pontiff. The city was illuminated for many nights as a sign of the general joy. The bells rang out again, the churches were opened, processions were renewed. The images of Our Lady began to gleam again.

After the return of Pius VII the cult of the street images of the Blessed Virgin flourished with new enthusiasm.

The number of shrines multiplied, and those which had been disfigured were made more beautiful. In every section of the city the people competed in adorning palaces and houses, streets and alleys with these signs of their faith.

The violence of 1870 renewed momentarily the injuries of the unbeliever to the street shrines. The *Voce della Verità* reported on August 29, 1873, that two of the Garibaldini, bent on mischief, went about saying: "If the Romans don't remove these dolls, we shall shatter them." Among the images that suffered damage at the hands of such as these were the shrine under the arch of the Biscione, that at Piazza della Pace, and that of Vicolo delle Bollette.

At one stage there was even a proposal made to remove all the effigies from public veneration; a petition was drawn up to the mayor of Rome, Count Luigi Pianciani, but without success. Many images had to be covered over, however, to spare them new profanation in the first years of the Savoy occupation of Rome.

With the passing of Papal Rome the number of street shrines constantly decreased. In 1853 when Alessandro Rufini wrote his *Indicazione delle Immagini di Maria SSma. Collocate sulle Mure Esterne di taluni Edifici dell'Alma Città di Roma* there were 1,421 street shrines dedicated to the Blessed Virgin, as well as another 1,318 images which had reference to other religious subjects. Now, despite the tremendous development of the city, there are only 535 street shrines in all.

Writing in 1939, Publio Parsi, to whose book *Edicole di Fede e di Pietà nelle vie di Roma* this article is almost totally indebted, laments the failure of the public builders in the Savoy and Fascist years of Rome's development to make any provision for this ancient Roman tradition in their modern buildings. One hears that since World War II new street shrines have appeared; those who love Rome will welcome such news if it be true.

Meanwhile, pilgrims to Rome for the Holy Year of 1950 will find at every turn these monuments of Roman faith and fervor. Certain of these in each section of the city deserve particular notice in a future article to appear in this review.

II

In visiting Rome during the Holy Year or in reflecting *in absentia* on the Eternal City, one can hardly do better than follow the order of F. Marion Crawford's chapters in *Ave Roma Immortalis* where the fourteen regions (*rioni, regiones*) of Rome provide the sequence of the book. Crawford writes:

> Here and there, in out-of-the-way places, overlooked in the modern rage for improvement, little marble tablets are set into the walls of old houses, bearing semi-heraldic devices such as a crescent, a column, a griffin, a stag, a wheel, and the like. Italian heraldry has always been eccentric and has shown a tendency to display all sorts of strange things, such as comets, trees, landscapes, and buildings in the escutcheon, and it would naturally occur to the stranger that the small marble shields, still visible here and there at the corners of old streets, must be the coats of arms of Roman families that held property in that particular neighborhood. But this is not the case. They are the distinctive devices of the fourteen rioni, or wards, into which the city was divided, with occasional modifications, from the time of Augustus to the coming of Victor Emmanuel, and which with some further changes survive to the present day. The tablets themselves were put up by Pope Benedict the Fourteenth, who reigned from 1740 to 1758 and who finally brought them up to the ancient number of fourteen; but from the Dark Ages the devices themselves were borne upon flags on all public occasions by the people of the different *regions*.[1]

This article was written for and published in the March 1950 issue of the *American Ecclesiastical Review*.

The *rioni*, therefore, have played a principal part in the history and life of Rome and correspond to something with deep roots and meaning in the *mores* of the Roman people. The modern development of the city has resulted in the addition of further regions to the traditional fourteen, and these, too, we must visit if our pilgrimage to the street shrines of Rome is to be complete.

But first of all it may be well to name the ancient *rioni*, indicating the numbers traditionally assigned to each:

I	Monti	VIII	Sant'Eustachio
II	Trevi	IX	Pigna
III	Colonna	X	Campitelli
IV	Campo Marzo	XI	Sant'Angelo
V	Ponte	XII	Ripa
VI	Parione	XIII	Trastevere
VII	Regola	XIV	Borgo

The street shrines of Rome are found in greatest number in these sections, but some interesting shrines may also be admired in the later sections of the city: Prati, Esquilino, Ludovisi, Celio, S. Saba, Castro Pretorio, Testaccio, and Sallustiano.

In his *Edicole di Fede e di Pietà nelle vie di Roma*, which is the principal source of these present notes, Publio Parsi enumerates some 530 street shrines, distributed among the Roman districts, ancient and modern, as follows: Trastevere 86; Monti 52; Parione 41; Ponte 37; Campo Marzo 32; Colonna 33; Campitelli 34; Regola 32; Trevi 24; S. Eustachio 24; Pigna 21; Borgo 18; Ripa 14; Prati 13; Esquilino 11; Ludovisi 9; Celio 9; S. Saba 10; S. Angelo 7; Castro Pretorio 7; Testaccio 6; Tiburtino 4; Sallustiano 2; Trionfale 2; Salario 2.

It will be noted that the fourteen more ancient districts, ᵻth the sole exception of Sant'Angelo, lead all the others in the numbers of their shrines. The relatively small number of those erected in Sant'Angelo is readily explained when we recall that the name of this district has nothing to do with the castle or the bridge but is derived from the church of the Holy Angel in Fish Market, in the heart of the old Ghetto.

If we begin our pilgrimage in the vast Monti section we are immediately reminded of the intensely *popular* origins of the Roman street shrines. The broad main streets of Monti were laid out in their present plan toward the end of the nineteenth century when there prevailed in Rome both a patriotism and a cosmopolitanism alien to those so long native to the Eternal City. The very names of Via Cavour and Via dell'Impero suffice to recall alike the recent history of the region and the changes of mood introduced by it.

Accordingly, it is through side streets, back streets, and even alleys that we must wander if we are to find either the people of Monti or the evidences of their devotion.

The neighborhood to the rear of St. John Lateran and particularly the narrow streets descending from the Lateran Hospital include many typical baroque shrines of the seventeenth century, as do also the crowded lanes around Madonna dei Monti and S. Agata de' Goti.

But perhaps the most appropriate shrine in Monti to single out for special comment is at the end of Via Baccina in the direction of Arco dei Pantani where we find ourselves before a poverty-stricken shrine which once knew days of greater splendor. In 1853 Rufini's book on Roman street shrines described this shrine:

> Near the building marked no. 1, belonging to Antonio Grassi, one notices a baldacchino of wood covered with lead, with pictures representing the Eternal Father an'

169

some cherubim and seraphim. This overlays a small marble temple, upheld by two columns, in the midst of which is a fresco of the Blessed Virgin with the Child on her knees and the inscription: "Purissimo Dei Genitricis cordi quod mens nostra amoris vulnere icta auspirat." A marble kneeler is in front of it; it features a sculptured sunburst, the center of which reproduces a heart with two kneeling seraphim at its sides, with the inscription: "The devotees of the Blessed Virgin of the Good Heart, 1838". A sea shell of marble for holy water may still be seen at one side. A tablet on the wall contains eighty-nine silver tokens and there are eight smaller tablets with records of graces received from God through the intercession of the miraculous image. The following inscription bears witness to the public devotion to Mary and of the spiritual treasures with which the Church wished to enrich her shrine: "His Holiness Pius VI, by decree of February 28, 1797, grants to all the faithful of both sexes an indulgence of 200 days, applicable also to the souls in purgatory, each time they devoutly and with hearts at least contrite recite the Litany of the Blessed Virgin before this sacred image."

Now all this spiritual grandeur has disappeared. Nothing remains but a simple modern frame around a ruined, retouched fresco; everything else has been corroded by neglect and by dampness. The face of the Madonna may still be discerned. It is turned slightly downward; the expression is thoughtful, and the Child, his head on the Virgin's shoulder, turns toward the observer. The design is good, revealing the capable hand of a talented artist, probably of the end of the sixteenth century. Many *ex-voti* still adorn the shrine. A bare electric bulb illumines one side and a few dry flowers add a pathetic touch. Beneath it there still survive two inscriptions: that of 1838, which recalls the restoration, and that of 1797, regarding the indulgences granted by Pope Pius VI.

In 1796 this image became the object of unusual public demonstrations following certain singular events which took place here on July 9 at the same time a strange movement of the eyes was observed at other street shrines in the city. At this image of Our Lady, called *La Madonna dell'Arco dei Pantani*, some lilies had been attached to the wall, and these, because of the length of the season and the constant beating down of the burning sun, had become dry branches, bare of every leaf and blossom. Suddenly it was observed that from these bunches of dry twigs three green clusters or natural buds, like those from which a lily flowers, had bloomed on the left side; another like them was seen to be budding on the other side. The four blossoms remained fresh, not for days, but for months, flourishing under the torrid July sun. The people became convinced that this was a supernatural sign exceeding any natural explanation, and as a result there followed repeated gatherings of crowds and a fervor in prayer before this shrine which were almost incredible.

Reference had already been made at least twice in these notes to seemingly miraculous phenomena in the case of certain of the *madonnelle* of Rome in July 1796. In all, some twenty-six street shrines have been the objects of ecclesiastical investigation with consequent declarations of the authenticity of the claims popularly made in their regard. Numerous others, similarly acclaimed by the populace, never received such official recognition. Noteworthy in connection with these prodigies is a decree of the Cardinal Vicar of the city dated February 28, 1797 which reveals the details of a careful canonical investigation conducted by Cardinal della Somaglia and his notary, Francesco Mari, into the claims of more than eighty-six witnesses who alleged that they had personally witnessed the wondrous evidence. The Decree of Approbation carefully notes that the investigations conducted by the Vicariate had not reached any conclusions with regard to some of the cases submitted, but it described the remarkable phenomena as having been "abundantly and more than abundantly confirmed" by the evidence submitted with respect to the following twenty-six images:

Madonna dell'Archetto
Addolorata degli Agonizzanti
Madonna del Vicolo delle Bollette
Madonna del Palazzo dell'Impresa Vecchia
Addolorata presso S. Andrea della Valle
Immacolata a S. Nicola de' Lorrnesi
Addolorata presso la Chiesa Nuova
SSmo. Crocifisso in Casa Pucci
Immacolata a S. Silvestro in Capite
Madonna del Cenacolo in S. Silvestro in Capite
Assunta alla Chiesa Nuova
Madonna della Lampada in S. Giovanni Calibita
Madonna delle Grazie in S. Maria della Consolazione
Madonna in Piazza dell'Olmo
Madonna del Rosario in Casa Galli
Madonna sotto l'Arco di Grotta Pinta
Madonna del Carmine a S. Martino ai Monti
Madonna del Carmine nella Cappella Interna del Noviziato
SSmo. Crocifisso in S. Giovanni in Ayno
(now at *Ss. Benedetto e Scolastica* in Via Torre
   Argentina)

Madonna del Rosario all'Arco della Ciambella
Madonna al Palazzo Odescalchi
Madonna sotto il Palazzo della Consulta
Madonna in Casa Bolognetti
Addolorata in Piazza Madama
(now in the church of S. Luigi dei Francesi)
Madonna di Guadalupe in S. Nicola in Carcere
Addolorata in Piazza del Gesù

In the heart of Trevi we find one of the shrines identified with this extraordinary history. In point of fact, two of the effigies most heralded by the Roman people in 1796 as instruments of divine wonders are found in Trevi. One of these, the *Madonna dell'Archetto*, is now housed in a graceful chapel of its own and is no longer, properly speaking, a *street shrine*. The owner was the once greatly beloved *Madonna del Vicolo delle Bollette*.

The shrine is now in a very neglected condition. A baldacchino with hangings protects a simple square wooden frame which encloses the image. A small marble shelf beneath it is crowded with vases of flowers; a candlestick emerges from them and holds a lighted bulb.

The painting is a worthy eighteenth-century canvas representing Our Lady in a mantle with large folds, her hands crossed on her breast and her eyes turned heavenward. Her face has an ecstatic expression, but the baroque artistry reflects scant spiritual insight. The rich colors impress the observer and give the shrine a strange fascination. A great many *ex-voti*, strings of coral, bracelets, and other votive offerings adorn the image. The shrine was once the property of a certain Domenico Bertagna, a kettlemaker on the Via delle Muratte.

Under the picture one finds the following inscript'
in stone: "Die IX Iulii 1796—Posuit oculum suum ◄

173

corda illorum ostendere illis magnalia operum Suorum."
This commemorates the events which give this shrine
a special place, together with the other twenty-five,
among the *madonnelle* of Rome.

The first witness at the eventual process of authentication was the Marquis del Bufalo, who, on his way to
the Via dell'Archetto to see the amazing things reported
as taking place there, had met the Marchioness Barbara
Palombara Massimi. She told him of other prodigies
announced in the Vicolo delle Muratte and advised him
to go there quickly since it was not yet crowded and so
that he might the more easily verify what was happening.

Del Bufalo's testimony is echoed in the contemporary
chronicles:

> The pupils of both the eyes of the image moved and
> turned upward so that little by little, very slowly, they
> became almost totally hidden under the upper eyelids.
> Then with the same slow movements they were lowered.
> This motion was so frequent that in the space of a quarter
> of an hour del Bufalo and the others present saw it
> repeated several times, the crowd meanwhile shouting,
> "*Evviva Maria*". "Look, she is moving her eyes!" and the
> like. Another time, as though animated, the eyes moved
> from one side to another almost as if to survey lovingly
> the bystanders and show that Mary heard with pleasure
> the praises which they were giving her. Other witnesses
> testified to having seen the eyes close completely and
> open again shortly after.

The records of the process show that these phenomena
occurred continually until November 25 of that same
year and that the glass in front of the image was frequently
moved to dispel the least suspicion of optical illusion.
the disorders of 1853 this shrine had a less edifying
. The image suffered vandalism on the night of

June 15 when its glass protecting cover was shattered and the image was robbed of the votive gifts which adorned it. As soon as the inhabitants of the vicinity discovered the sacrilege, they not only decided to adorn the image with other jewels but they restored the shrine completely. In reparation for the outrage, the image was carried in procession to the nearby church of S. Maria in Via where a solemn triduum was held. It was then returned to its street shrine "with great display of lights and crowds of people".

There are more than a score of other street shrines in the crowded Trevi section. Nearby, the Colonna region rejoices in more than thirty, of which perhaps the best known of those dedicated to the Madonna is that found where the Via dei Cappuccini crosses the Via della Purificazione. Here we find a tabernacle very modest in physical fabric but enriched by much popular devotion. A small roof protects a poor wooden frame which contains a venerated image of the Blessed Virgin with her Divine Son. The Child stands on Mary's knee and holds in one hand a cross which rests upon His shoulder. The painting, done in the eighteenth century, is in no way exceptional, but numberless *ex-voti* of every kind reveal the spiritual indebtedness of the Roman people to this shrine, more significant in its poverty than many artistically more notable objects of devotion.

Less than a century ago the Campo Marzo region numbered fully a hundred street shrines. No section of modern Rome has seen so much reconstruction, however, with a consequent destruction of innumerable older houses, narrow streets, and now forgotten little squares. With the passing of these, Rome lost more than three score *madonnelle* in Campo Marzo alone.

Of the more than thirty shrines remaining, several of

the best are on Via del Babuino. Perhaps the most conspicuous, however, is the shrine on Via S. Sebastianello beyond Piazza di Spagna and along the wall under the Pincio.

Here on the high wall we find an unusual shrine, composed of elements of different epochs resulting in a very interesting whole. A modern frame in Renaissance style surrounds a square niche, to the back of which is attached a piece of sixteenth-century sculpture. It is a matronly figure of the Blessed Mother holding the Divine Child in her arms. It is sculptured by the strong, sure hands of a capable artist, a follower of Sansovino. On the border of the frame is carved the salutation "Ave Maria", and to one side is a strange detail, a miniature Venetian balcony, delicately carved to serve as a flower vase. Some small pictures and *ex-voti* surround the image, and an iron arm upholds a votive lamp.

Unlike Campo Marzo, Ponte tenaciously retains its ancient picturesque character, and among its thirty-seven street shrines one particularly deserves notice. It is one of a half dozen or so shrines on Via dei Coronari and rises imposingly on stone blocks at the corner of Vicolo Domizio. Two columns with artificial capitals uphold a triangular architrave, in the frieze of which is the inscription: "Instaurata fuit quam cernis Pontis Imago", while the base reads: "Albertus Serra de Monte Ferrato". Simple and classic in its severe lines, the work is accredited to Antonio da Sangallo, who designed it in the first half of the sixteenth century at the order of Cardinal Alberto Serra di Monferrato. Sangallo, according to Vasari, chose Perin del Vaga to paint the picture, the *Imago Pontis*, on the interior wall of the niche. This was undoubtedly a substitution for a more ancient image of which records speak as far back as 1463.

The painting by Perin del Vaga, representing the Coronation of the Virgin, is now almost completely obliterated. Through the withe which protects it there may be faintly glimpsed the faded traces of the figures of the Redeemer and Our Lady and other confused traces of color. A gilded frame surrounds the almost totally lost painting. Above, over the shrine, window frames and escutcheons contribute to a general scene of remarkable artistic interest.

Parione offers several noteworthy public shrines, most familiar of which are doubtless those of *S. Maria dell'Anima* and the elaborate, monumental shrine of *Piazza dell'Orologio*. But of its two score shrines the most *popular* is quite probably that on the side of the archway which opens on the street along the side of the church of *S. Maria in Vallicella*. Here one finds a wooden tabernacle in the form of a square niche with a grilled door and a frame surmounted by a baldacchino–like crown. Two heads of cherubim soar above the figure; another is under the shrine; two angels float on clouds at the sides. In the niche itself is a canvas representing Christ Crucified between Our Lady and St. John, a mediocre painting from the end of the eighteenth century or the beginning of the nineteenth. But to the fore is a charming sixteenth–century group in carved wood, with a polychrome statue of Mary. The Blessed Virgin extends her arms to open her mantle and enfold it on three religious, seen in prayer at her feet. Her eyes are lowered; the expression of her face is almost a smile. A silver crown reposes on her head and about the shrine there are vases of flowers and many *ex-voti*.

At one time this tabernacle must have been on the opposite side of the arch, where a marble tablet may st be seen with the inscription: "Alms of those dev to Mary". Perhaps the image was transferred after a miracle attributed to this shrine on the fated Saturday which was July 1, 1796. The chronicle records:

> The sacred eyelids, which the artist had carved as lowered, slowly lifted in the same manner as human eyes when a person opens them. And this opening was so much more evident and marvelous that in its case the whole eyeball was uncovered and the entire pupil acquired a certain brightness and—as others said—an extraordinary sparkle resembling the brightness of the eye of a healthy, vivacious person. The movement, repeated several times in a short while, was slow and steady; the eyes, as they were uncovered, acquiring the gleam of a gem struck by light.

So great was the impression produced by this extraordinary event that a young worker, affected by what he had seen, fell on his knees, crying: "Ah, Holy Mother, you have saved my soul! Without this, tomorrow I might have been in the depths of hell!"

Of some twenty-five shrines on the streets of Regola (including one of singularly imposing proportions enshrining the emblem of the Monte di Pietà, the image of Our Blessed Redeemer, and dominating Piazza del Monte di Pietà), the one which Parsi describes as "spiritually most important" is on Via dei Cappellari, not far from Piazza Campo de Fiori.

It is an eighteenth-century tabernacle, surrounded by ornamental detail in plaster, reproducing in bas-relief garlands of flowers, lilies, leaves, and shells. The work is not remarkable, but the total impression is pleasing. The painting, representing the Blessed Virgin, is very faded, but it is surrounded by many *ex-voti* which appear to be constantly augmented. On a small stone slab beneath near the words: "Tota pulchra es et macula non est in Fr. Francesco Baldissoni and other witnesses asserted that on the famed July 9, 1796, the sacred image opened and closed its eyes many times and continued to move them for several days. No process of authentication was undertaken in the case of this shrine, however.

The most important Marian shrine of the S. Eustachio section is situated on the facade of a private home in Piazza della Rotonda. It is an eighteenth-century fresco of large proportions, surrounded by a baroque frame with plaster spiral curves and surmounted by a dove, the symbol of the Holy Ghost, on a sunburst. The painting represents the Immaculate Conception. Portraying her arms crossed on her breast and her glance lowered, the image of Mary has something almost *aerial* about it, pervaded as it is by a quality of movement lent it by the flowing of the mantle, widening at the bottom in large swirls and seeming to lift the figure into space. A winged angel leans toward Mary, while other heads of angels make a crown for her. Unfortunately, the picture is now somewhat faded, and its colors are no longer clear, though one still senses the original beauty of the painting.

Two of the images authenticated with reference to the prodigies of July 1796 are still venerated in the Pigna section. On Via dell'Arco della Ciambella are the ruins of the Terme di Agrippa, on the pagan walls of which, as if to redeem them and to testify to the triumph of Christianity, was erected a sacred shrine dedicated to the Blessed Virgin. Apart from its interesting history, this shrine has the most valuable artistic merit of the street shrines in Pigna.

A sixteenth-century marble tabernacle, composed of two pilasters with composite capitals supporting an architrave, rests on an altarlike marble table supported by two brackets trimmed with acanthus leaves. Between the two brackets there is a head of a cherub. The pilasters and the architrave are decorated with floral and ornamental detail sculptured in bas-relief. Inside the tabernacle is a marble frame with a small head of an angel in its center. This, in turn, encloses a smaller gilded frame, within which is the image of Our Lady. The tabernacle is surmounted by two plaster angels holding a crown of flowers and by a huge wooden baldacchino. On the bottom part is a marble slab on which another image of Mary is sculptured with the following inscription: "He who ponders and meditates on your mysteries, O Blessed Virgin, lifts to you chaste thoughts, and you enkindle love in his soul the while he innocently offers his heart." A marble kneeler is attached to the altar, and the latter is modestly furnished: Wooden candlesticks and vases with flowers, and two lanterns, held by iron brackets, burn constantly.

The shrine was completed toward the end of the eighteenth century by the Capparucci family which for more than a century had inhabited a house nearby. They refashioned in tabernacle form an ornamental frame which the Capparucci themselves, who were stonecutters by profession, had perhaps owned. The lovely frame, worked with elegant borders of the sixteenth century, must have been executed by a competent artist.

In older times the shrine protected a canvas of the *Madonna of the Rosary*, restored in 1830 by the painter Marcucci. This was another image which in 1796 produced the prodigy of the movement of the eyes. The chronicle declares concerning it:

A fine artist, who was devoted to the image and had taken care of it for a long time, having heard on July 9 of the prodigies that were being manifested at other shrines, left his carving shop, located nearby, to observe one of the marvels. Passing in front of this shrine, he noticed a spiderweb on the front of it and, taking a ladder, climbed up to clean the glass with his handkerchief. Another person, standing below, suddenly called his attention to evidence of a miracle, which he observed, in the form of the opening and closing of Mary's eyes. And in fact, looking at the left eye, which is turned on the Child, instead of seeing it opened, as it is always, he saw it completely closed, the upper lid having fallen on the lower. Recitations of the Litany, weeping and shouting from the spectators, the arrival of a crowd of more than two hundred persons happened in a flash. And all became witnesses of the prodigy, which was repeated time and again: The eyelids of both eyes of the Virgin, lowering with slow motion, showed a perfect closing so that the entire eyeball, the white as well as the dark part of the pupil, was covered; and after remaining so for the space of an *Ave Maria*, they opened with more rapid motion than that with which they closed. From two o'clock that first morning, until late into the night, it continued that way, and on the following days, at least, for the three weeks of which there was written evidence of the process, the applauding people invoked and attested to that same amazing closing and opening of the sacred eyes. His Excellency, Duke Lante was one of those who checked the more carefully by climbing a ladder which had been left at the shrine for that purpose, as did the lawyer Celestini. At close range they were able to witness repeatedly the remarkable portent. Very plainly they also saw the eyeball move, with the pupil shifting from side to side, as if to look at the bystanders, and then clearly rise and lower; the face became beautiful and lifelike in that heavenly motion.

It is easy to imagine with what jealous solicitude th image was tended by the Capparucci family, who, besi* beautifying the shrine, kept a light always burning before it and on the first Sunday in October celebrated a solemn feast there, decorating the shrine and the street around it with hangings of myrtle and of lights.

In 1873 the miraculous image was robbed of its *ex-voti* by sacrilegious hands, and from that time on, for fear of other acts of the vandalism common in that period, the Capparucci family removed the painting from the shrine every evening, substituting a slab with the name of Mary inscribed on it. When they later moved to another location, they carried the image away with them, leaving the shrine abandoned. A carpenter of the neighborhood, in order to fill the empty space, engaged the painter Pietro Campofiorito to make another copy of the ancient Madonna, and this was placed in the shrine some time in December 1895.

The neighborhood around the church of S. Maria in Campitelli is rich in shrines. Indeed, many houses are decorated with the maiolica polychrome discs which commemorate the celebration throughout Campitelli in 1924 of the fourteenth centenary of the apparition of Mary to a Roman patrician woman who was feeding the poor at her palace gate. On every side the walls of houses are imbedded with these miniature shrines recalling the visit of *S. Maria in Portico*.

Of the numerous notable street shrines in Campitelli, one in particular attracts us with its tabernacle, pictures, and inscriptions covering the entire outer curve of the apse of the church of *S. Maria della Consolazione*. It commemorates the deliverance of the city from pestilance in 1658.

The principal figure is modelled on that of a woman of ⸱ people, with large eyes and imposing appearance.

The Child in her lap lifts his arm in a gesture of benediction. It is a seventeenth-century painting and is executed with a bold brush in almost sculptural relief.

The image is enclosed in a marble baroque frame on which is inscribed "Consolatrix Afflictorum—Anno Salutis 1658". The tabernacle is surmounted by a wooden baldacchino and surrounded by clouds painted on the wall from which heads of cherubim emerge and a large sunburst radiates. Under the frame is a stone tablet held up by several iron spiral curves.

On a small stone is the inscription, "Redemptori ac Sanctissimae Eius Genitrici Mariae Urbe e Pestilentia Liberata Gloria Sempiterna."

Below this was placed in 1787 one of those admonitory inscriptions which in their forthright simplicity reveal the homely faith of the Roman people: "Pause here, passerby, and bow your head humbly! Here is the Source of Graces; this is the Mother of God. Look at her, weep, and pray—for she does not refuse graces to those devoted to her."

The *rione* S. Angelo includes the ancient Ghetto of the Roman Jews. Most mysterious of its labyrinth of streets and alleys is the Via delle Botteghe Oscure. A private dwelling on the corner between the Caetani Palace and the Piazza Paganica displays the modest shrine of another of the twenty-six *miraculous* images of 1796.

Meager in proportions, the shrine is bare of ornamental display. To its simplicity, however, there is added a touch of eighteenth-century elegance which makes it especially attractive. Under the picture there are two lilies of plaster entwined and tied by a ribbon of the same unfortunate material. The base of the tabernacle is formed by a bracket, also of plaster, with an inscription on the front which curves over the sides: "Mater Providentiae". A baldacchino of iron plate surmounts the shrine. The painting represents the Blessed Virgin at half-bust with her hands on her breast and her eyes lowered and is a work of the eighteenth century. The workmanship is quite fine especially in the delicate manner in which the features of the face are suffused with truly celestial sweetness.

Below, embedded in the wall, is a large marble tablet on which is inscribed the following:

I.H.S.

QUAM VENERARIS IMAGO

CUM SEPT. ID. IUL. AN. CI 1796

VARIO OCULORUM MOTU PROPITIO ASPECTU

SUPPLICEM POPULUM REFICERET

OMNIUM CORDA SIBI DEMERUIT ET EX CORDE LAUDES

HOC AMOR M.P.

A number of contemporary shrines, chiefly fashioned of ceramic, bring refreshing color to the modern residential sections of Ripa, especially the streets sloping down the Aventine toward Via del Mare from Piazza S. Anselmo and the noble Piazza dei Cavalieri di Malta. But it is to Tiber Island that we must turn for the most venerable of the street shrines of Ripa.

Just beyond the pharmacy of the Hospital of the Brothers of St. John of God we see a wooden tabernacle containing a recent reproduction of a very old miraculous image of *Santa Maria Cantu-Fluminis*, popularly called *La Madonna della Lampada*. The original was painted around 1290 and is still venerated at the first altar on the right in the adjoining church of S. Giovanni Calabita. The popular name, *della Lampada*, seems to come from a miracle worked in 1557, when the image, at that time in a small niche near the river, was submerged by the waters of the Tiber without being harmed, in fact without its lamp being extinguished.

For the many miracles associated with it, the image was crowned by the Vatican Chapter on March 19, 1664. On July 9, 1796, it was one of the images reported to have opened its eyes and moved them toward the people. It is among the twenty-six images approved after the canonical examination into the alleged incidents.

The overcrowded workers' quarters of Trastevere are by all odds the most generously provided with these outdoor evidences of Roman faith and popular fervor. More than fourscore street shrines, ranging from humble images to ornate public altars, may be found in the *rione*. Most remarkable is the facade of a small house on Via dei Cascellari, entirely taken up by an imposing shrine in neoclassic style. A large baldacchino in the form of a cupola covers a marble tabernacle constructed of two columns resting on a bracket and holding a triangular architrave. In the center there is a nineteenth-century painting of Our Lady with the Child surrounded by several saints. On the border of the frame an inscription reads: "Mother of Providence, pray for us."

Last of the traditional *rioni*, Borgo lost several of her best known shrines when the *spina* was demolished just over a decade ago. The remaining street shrines, if of lesser artistic merit, are nonetheless the objects of that even greater piety which we instinctively expect in the shadow of St. Peter's cupola.

As soon as we pass the Porta di S. Spirito, near a secondary entrance to the hospital, we find on Via dei Penitenzieri the most notable shrine of this section. It is baroque tabernacle of marble, severe in its lines. Under its bracket there is a charming angel head, with festoons and the inscription: "Anno Dni 1665". The central image is a good, though somewhat highly colored, painting of the Blessed Virgin in large proportions, her hands crossed on her breast and her gaze turned upward. On the frame is the inscription: "Sub tuum praesidium". Many *ex-voti* surround the image. A small lamp hangs from a wrought iron bracket, and on the altar before the shrine there is a constant renewal of fresh flowers from the hospital staff and relatives of the sick. It is one of the most touching focal points of Roman devotion.

Of the more modern *rioni* and their public shrines little need be noted. The shrines themselves are less numerous and, of course, almost completely contemporary in their inspiration. Most, though not all, are on buildings housing religious orders or institutions. Typical of the shrines in the Esquiline region, however, is one near 161 Via Merulana in the low wall which borders the sidewalk. A wide square niche, enclosed by a grille and surrounded by a plaster frame, protects a nineteenth-century canvas of the *Madonna del Carmelo*. Around it are numerous holy pictures of all sizes and styles, together with *ex-voti* and a profusion of flowers, all revealing the popular veneration in which the image is locally held.

There are about nine shrines in the fashionable Ludovisi section. Noteworthy is a lovely nineteenth-century medallion in marble, surrounded by heads of angels. It is located on the corner of Via Emilia and Via Lazio. In its center is a gracious Madonna with the Holy Child in her arms, delicately sculptured. Before it there is a lamp of wrought iron.

Much admired in the *rione* Sallustiano is a modern sculptured shrine on the corner of Via Quintino Sella and Via Flavia. It reproduces a charming Madonna with the Child in her arms. On its marble base is the inscription: "Beata Mater".

A modern business district, lining the Via Nazionale, cuts through the *rione* Castro Pretorio. The street shrines of this district are therefore few and, on the whole, not impressive. Perhaps the most attractive is a modern medallion with a frame decorated with angel heads at the corner of Via Nazionale and Via Torino. It supports a delicate sculpture representing Our Lady and the Divine Child. An arm of wrought iron holds a small lamp which casts a benign light on the strolling couples of this least Roman of streets.

The Celian region has several interesting shrines, again particularly on the older streets as Via della Navicella and Via di S. Stefano Rotondo. There is a baroque shrine of the Redeemer in Piazza dei Ss. Giovanni e Paolo and another of Saint Gregory the Great not far away. Best known of the *madonnelle* in this section is on Via della Valle delle Camene, a chapellike shrine encased at the top of the wall surrounding a private property. Through a barred window one may glimpse a small interior damaged by time and dampness. In the midst of candleholders and *ex-voti* on the altar is a sixteenth-century fresco of Our Lady of Good Counsel. On one side of a window there is a tablet with the following inscription: "Whoever prays before this image will gain 100 days indulgence, by decree of His Holiness Pius VII, July 13, 1803." The same inscription appears on a marble tablet across the front of the little chapel.

Almost all the street shrines of Testaccio are modern reproductions of the very ancient venerated image of S. Maria Liberatrice. Some of them have been erected in the last two decades. Typical is a beautiful baroque shrine at the corner of Via Galileo Ferraris and Via Beniamino Franklin. The central medallion is surmounted by charming heads of angels under an arch, while below there are lilies entwined in spirals about a slab with the inscription: "S. Maria Liberatrice". The picture in the medallion is a reproduction of the original image so much loved in the region and was painted on canvas about twenty years ago by Professor Capanni.

The front of a small house situated between the two archways of the Porta S. Paolo in the San Saba region is decorated with two identical shrines decorated with the heads of cherubim and entwined lilies. The plaster parts are well sculptured, and, although the frescoes are now badly faded, one still notices their skillful design and the warmth which enlivens them. One represents the Annunciation; the other, the Blessed Virgin with her Child and a saint in prayer before them.

The vast majority of the public shrines of the Prati streets are modern *maiolica*, imitations in most cases of della Robbia type medallions. On the Via Vittoria Colonna, however, near the Lungotevere dei Mellini there is a charming marble image of the Virgin and Child, done in bas-relief.

Not at all to be compared with the shrines in the public thoroughfares of the *rioni* of Rome are the half dozen or so shrines to be found in the so-called *quartieri* of the modern city: Salario, Tiburtino, and Trionfale. A certain antique charm still hovers about a Madonna of Good Counsel at the corner of Via Candia and Via Leone IV in

Trionfale; it dates from the seventeenth century and is one of the two shrines in the quarter. Tiburtino offers four shrines, the best a *Salve Regina* of the 1800s in Piazzale Franco Baldini.

Greatest of the shrines in the *quartieri* and majestic among all the public shrines of Rome is the glittering mosaic of the regally enthroned Madonna which looks out along the Via Nomentana from the lofty wall of Porta Pia. Its princely Child holds the globe in one hand while He blesses with the other. Originally a painting by Capparoni (1831–1907), commissioned in 1862 by the architect entrusted by Pius IX with the restoration of the great gate of Pius IV, the *Madonna of Porta Pia* suffered the ravages of seventy-five years' rain and sun and had virtually disappeared by 1938. In that year local parish priests, aided generously by the Italian civil authorities, sponsored the reproduction of the painting in mosaic, a heroic work achieved in the Vatican studios under the direction of Professor Biagio Biagetti.

The present brilliant shrine, tremendous in proportions and effect, sheds its luminous benediction on a city gate about which the last decades of the nineteenth century had cast many and sad shadows.

Lovers of Rome and of the sacred shrines of the Eternal City would doubtless protest against a failure to mention in these sketchy notes those Roman street shrines which are now preserved for veneration in chapels of their own. The first article in this series recalled some former street shrines which have been transported for more systematic cult into chapels of nearby parish or collegiate churches. But quite special is the case and the history of *le cappelle*, a cherished group apart.

189

Alumni of the North American College will remember with special devotion *La Madonna dell'Archetto* and *La Madonna del Divino Amore*. The *cappelle* of these devotional favorites of the American *Romani*, as well as the chapels of *Le Madonne del Soccorso*, *del Buon Consiglio*, and *del'Arco Oscuro*, all beloved of the *Romani di Roma*, deserve later and separate Holy Year notes of their own.[2]

III

We have already recalled in these Holy Year notes some of the street shrines of Rome which have long since been translated into nearby churches for more systematic care and supervised cult. Typical of these, as noted in our first installment of notes, may be mentioned the *Madonna della Strada*, venerated in the Gesù, the renowned church of the Jesuit Fathers.

A group apart among the street shrines are those which are enshrined in wayside chapels of their own, *cappelle*, erected usually under private auspices or through the devotion of confraternities of a local and popular kind. Traditionally beloved by the Roman people are five wayside chapels dedicated to the Blessed Mother: the Madonnas *dell'Arco Oscuro*, *del Soccorso*, *del Buon Consiglio*, *del Divino Amore*, and *dell'Archetto*.

The chapel of the *Madonna dell'Arco Oscuro* is located in Villa Giulia beneath an ancient passageway, recently closed, which was called the *arco oscuro* because of its darkness and its associations. The precincts of the passageway were the object of the well-founded fears of wayfarers, and many and lurid were the tales of violence and peril at the hands of outlaws told of the *arco oscuro*.

An image of the Blessed Mother was erected for veneration in the shadows of the dark passage and straightway edifying accounts of deliverances from evil as well as conversions to grace began to compete in number and drama with the whispered tales of evil. Those whom business brought into the neighborhood of the Dark Arch became the devout clients of the *Madonna dell'Arco Oscuro*. In the last decade of the eighteenth

This article was written for and published in the April 1950 issue of the *American Ecclesiastical Review*.

century the shrine became the particular charge of a hermit, Fra Giovanni, who undertook to provide for its shelter a worthy chapel, the origins of which are commemorated in an inscription still to be seen on the inner wall.

Parsi quotes a daybook of the ordinariate wherein are described the circumstances of the completion of the chapel. Apparently Fra Giovanni did with his own hands the initial work of building and beautifying the shrine. Contributions were speedily forthcoming once the work was underway, and apparently the workers in the vineyards nearby were foremost among the benefactors. The zealous interest of the parish priest of S. Maria del Popolo, within whose jurisdiction the region lies, made possible a temporary transfer of the image to that historic church while the work was in progress and also a particularly impressive blessing of the finished chapel on December 7, 1797.

On the vigil of Christmas 1797 (a Sunday), a solemn procession from S. Maria del Popolo escorted the picture of the Madonna back to its proper place in the *arco oscuro*. The contemporary report speaks of the length and erudition of the pastor's sermon, delivered from a pulpit erected outside the new chapel. It records how many and fervent were the litanies chanted and the hymns sung, nor does it neglect to mention a concert of wind instruments provided by a Roman band which had enlivened yet more the popular procession. The blessing with a relic of the Virgin, followed by a display of fireworks, terminated the era of dark deeds associated with the passageway and inaugurated the pacific reign of the Madonna over the isolated, lonely region.

The following morning a solemn Mass was sung before the shrine, the first Mass to be offered in the new *cappella*. Fra Giovanni, greatly encouraged in his work by this popular and official patronage, pressed for further embellishments of the chapel. Distinguished Roman citizens, foremost among them the Duchess Braschi, so generously furnished the little sanctuary that in the early part of the nineteenth century it was a jewel of Roman homage to the Blessed Mother.

In more recent years the passageway of the *arco oscuro* was closed, but the chapel of the Madonna still stands. Its entrance is closed by massive iron gates, and the interior is neglected and damp. Sadly faded images of saints still relieve the bareness of the walls, as do a number of votive gifts, among them an old pistol and a crutch. Over the altar a cheap reproduction of the original image is displayed in a tawdry frame as if to preserve by prescription the rights of the *Madonna dell'Arco Oscuro* to her place in Villa Giulia. The original, the Madonna holding her Child with St. Joseph by her side, has been temporarily removed to a nearby home lest it deteriorate even further, pending a possible restoration of the chapel.

Sometime after the middle of the eighteenth century (perhaps shortly after 1759) the Roman public institution for charitable loans, the famed Monte di Pietà, erected the chapel of the *Madonna del Soccorso* on Via Giovanni Berta. The shrine was doubtless intended to pay homage to the Blessed Mother under a title appropriate to work of the sponsoring patrons and consistent with the errands which brought so many destitute into the streets around the Monte di Pietà.

The chapel closes a blind alley hard by the headquarters of the charitable loan association as these were enlarged in 1759. The original image is now venerated at the side altar of Saint Matthew in the nearby church of the Trinità dei Pellegrini, whither it was removed as a res of the vandalism so flagrant in the period 1870–80. A copy of the Madonna, a Virgin with the Child, one arm lifted in blessing, has been enshrined in the *cappella* since the 1890s when the Monte di Pietà restored and enlarged the chapel after a period of abandonment identified with the disorders mentioned.

It is easy to distinguish the features added to the chapel at the end of the nineteenth century from the essential aspects present since the beginning. Save for the difference in the actual image and for the disappearance of the two side canvasses and the outside kneelers, the wayside chapel may still be recognized from the description written in 1853 by Rufini in *Indicazione delle Immagini di Maria SSma. Collocate sulle Mure Esterne di taluni Edifici dell'Alma Città di Roma*:

> Under the arch of the Monte di Pietà there is a small chapel restored in this current year with paintings, stuccos, golden and other decorations. Over the large cornice one reads, "Sancta Maria Succurre Miseris", and the whole is covered by a small wooden ceiling. In the inside turn there is painted the holy name of Mary. There is also a small altar of marble and, sustained by stucco seraphim, a canvas image of *Maria Santissima del Soccorso* with the Divine Child in her arms. Both heads are adorned with small silver crowns. Over the frame there are three stucco cherubs in adoration. On the side walls may be seen two canvases which represent the *Adoration of the Magi* and the *Presentation in the Temple*. Within the chapel are found two marble kneelers; two similar ones are found outside. Rich gifts give token of the special devotion of the faithful. The chapel is guarded by iron gates.

On Via Tor de' Conti, in front of the walls that circle he Forum of Augustus, there was built in 1834 a chapel in honor of the *Madonna del Buon Consiglio*. This chapel was built through the generosity of the Stubinetti family whose properties in that district were crossed by a narrow road considered very dangerous and unpleasant, especially at night. The family eventually obtained permission to close the road and to erect a wayside chapel for the public veneration of a Madonna hitherto privately cherished in their home.

The chapel is closed by an iron gate, and in the frieze of the neoclassic portal is inscribed the title, *Mater Boni Consilii*. On one side there still remains a marble slab with a petition for alms to replenish with oil the lamp before the Madonna.

In recent times the interior has been reduced in height and the chapel has thereby lost its earlier dignity, being now somehow stunted in appearance. The walls are bare and bleached. In the center background is a small altar and a richly carved wooden recess containing a canvas dating from the end of the eighteenth or the beginning of the nineteenth century. It reproduces a delicate likeness of the Mother of Good Counsel.

To one side may be seen a large crucifix and a small statue of St. Anthony. Two kneelers are provided before the altar. On a side wall there is the following inscription: "In onore della miracolosa Vergine del Buon Consiglio i benefattori fedeli accolgono la di lei festa con omaggio e devozione il 26 maggio, 1884, primo cinquantesimo in cui fu messa in questa veneranda cappella.—Il custode Amadio Paoloni."

A stone slab records the indulgences attached to this chapel by Pope Gregory XVI in a decree of June 11, 1834. Its unusual spiritual privileges enhanced popular esteem for the *cappella* of the *Madonna del Buon Consiglio*, and until very recent years it was constantly adorned with *ex-voti* left by innumerable devout clients.

Two of the Madonnas enshrined in their own wayside chapels are identified with the strange happenings of July 9, 1796, among *le madonnelle* of Rome. In our second installment of these notes we mentioned the case of the *Madonna dell'Archetto*, and to this particularly hallowed shrine we must shortly return. The same fateful date features in the history of the *Madonna del Divino Amore*.

This wayside shrine on Via dei Prefetti will not, of course, be confused with the shrine of the *Madonna del Divino Amore* in the Roman *campagna* to which so many tens of thousands come in pilgrimage from the *castelli Romani* and from Rome itself each year at Pentecost. The latter sanctuary, familiar to alumni of the North American College, is strangely majestic in its primitive simplicity, a supernatural oasis in the rude wastes of the *campagna*.[1]

In his account written in 1853 Rufini mentions the *cappella* on Via dei Prefetti as being "under the madhouse attached to Rome's lunatic asylum . . . a small shrine with an iron gate where one may venerate an image of the Madonna under the title of Divine Love."

The application of this mystic title of Our Lady to the present image appears to be due to the patronage of the original shrine by a pious group which flourished in Rome during the early sixteenth century, the so-called Company of Divine Love. The devout confraternity held its meetings in the parish church of S. Nicola dei Prefetti, and the shrine in all probability takes its name from association with them.

The chapel itself is unadorned, but the principal feature, the canvas of the Madonna, is of more than usual artistic

196

interest. A seventeenth-century painting, it has even been attributed to Sassoferrato and is certainly the work of an accomplished craftsman. The figure of Mary is represented at half-bust; the colorings (rose and azure dominate) are good, and a genuine spirit of recollection in prayer is achieved by such details as the lowered eyes, the serene countenance, and the gently folded hands of the Madonna.

A modern marble altar and a profusion of *ex-voti*, together with an unduly ornate *sunburst*, set off the image itself which, as we have remarked, was reported by many faithful as reproducing the phenomena of the movement of the eyes on July 9, 1796. No official confirmation of these particular claims, however, was made in the subsequent vicariate decree concerning other shrines in the city.

More fortunate in the results of its canonical investigation in 1796 and by all odds the most popular and faithfully preserved of Roman *cappelle* is that of the *Madonna dell'Archetto*. There is probably no priest educated at the nearby North American College who has not at one time or another in his student days joined with the curious little group of devout Romans who assemble in this chapel at stated hours and seasons for litanies to the Blessed Mother of the Small Arch.

The image venerated in this uniquely beautiful shrine dates from sometime around 1690. It is painted in oil on tile and is the work of a Bolognese artist, Domenico Muratori, of the school of Caracci. It was originally commissioned by Marchesa Alessandra Millini Muti Savorelli Papazzuri who desired a copy of a Madonna in the convent of the Cappuccine delle Barberine.

Muratori's copy was placed within a niche under an

archway between the Palazzo Casati and an adjoining religious house in an alley connecting Via di S. Marcello with Via dell'Archetto. From the name of the latter narrow street, the crowded neighborhood and its beloved shrine both take their local names.

From the first days of its erection in the alley by Palazzo Casati this privileged *madonnella* was destined to play a conspicuous part in the popular religious life of Rome. By the middle of the eighteenth century devotion to this street shrine had so flourished that it seemed wise to public authorities to erect iron gates at each end of the passageway. These were closed each evening after *Ave Maria* in order to protect by night the accumulation of precious *ex-voti* surrounding the image of Mary.

In 1751 the niche protecting the painting was considerably embellished by the plasterer Ferrari and the sculptor Grassi with offerings contributed by the thousands of pious persons who regularly visited the *Madonna dell'Archetto* at all hours, in all times, over a period of years.

It was probably no surprise to the Roman people to learn that the first of the street shrine prodigies reported in the city July 9, 1796, was connected with the *Madonna dell'Archetto*. Parsi reprints an eyewitness account of these first extraordinary occurrences. It was related by a certain Antonio Ambrosini who chanced to pass through the neighborhood at about noontime of that eventful day. He heard someone assert that the eyes of the nearby image of the Madonna had been seen to close and to reopen in unmistakable fashion.

Ambrosini betook himself immediately to the shrine and found it still possible, the report having not yet spread, to examine the picture closely and carefully. A few other citizens were standing close by him, minutely observing the features of the Madonna, when suddenly Ambrosini was rewarded with a stupendous spectacle concerning which he later made the following sworn deposition:

> I observed that no longer could the light be seen from both eyes but that unmistakably the upper lid had lowered and united with the lower eyelid so that it presented a perfect closing of the eyes. I confess that in truth I was so shaken that I thought the distance was deceiving me and that my eyes were seeing imperfectly. Wherefore I took particular care to check my faculties of sight, and I quickly placed my hands on my own eyes. I closed these for a very brief moment, and then once again I reopened them, fixing them on the eyes of *Maria Santissima*. I then saw very well that these continued to remain shut, but in the next instant they opened, and the upper eyelids returned to their place so that once again I saw the light from those holy eyes. And this movement of the eyes was so visible and so clear that I cannot describe it better than by saying that the holy image made a very wide opening of its eyes. Upon beholding such a marvel I could not refrain from lifting my voice, and I gave out a very loud cry. I cannot recall the words I said inasmuch as my being was so completely shaken and my body *frozen*; at the same time I was so stirred that spontaneous tears came to my eyes. Cries similar to mine came from the few people who were present, since they, too, were witnesses to the same miracle as I saw. As soon as the wonder became known, crowds began to come and this continued for weeks and months. From the first sign of dawn until late at night crowds gathered in such manner as to require a military guard in many places, and as all Rome knew, throughout July and a good part of August, it was necessary to restrain the people in the one direction as far

as the corner of Piazza S. Apostoli and in the other direction as far as the Oratorio di S. Marcello so that with good order everyone succeeded in approaching, little by little, the Arch.

One of the principal witnesses heard in the eventual canonical process conducted by the Vicariate was Fra Giovenale Goani of the Franciscan Conventuals in nearby Santi Apostoli. Skeptical of the reports he had heard concerning the *miracle*, he visited the shrine, only to change his opinion.

Again we are indebted to Parsi for an eyewitness report, this time as given by Fra Giovenale:

> I remained in the same place, determined to stay for three or four hours so that I might attest that however long a time I stayed I could not confirm the marvel that was being universally sung. Suddenly, when I was hardly thinking of it, yet was standing there with my eyes fixed on those of the Virgin Mary, I saw clearly an obvious movement in both the holy eyes. I observed that the eyeballs moved while the pupils were gradually raised, then almost totally concealed under the upper eyelids so that the dark pupils no longer could be seen. Then I noticed that after a brief space of time the pupils lowered slowly and returned to their proper position. . . . The movement of the pupils up and down was accomplished with much grace and majesty so that, although it excited devotion, faith, and tenderness, it imposed at the same time a real respect and veneration which touched all hearts.
>
> In the same instant in which I myself saw this miraculous movement, the spectators around me confirmed it with cries, tears, and loud rejoicing, as they beheld so moving a spectacle, exclaiming: *"Evviva Maria!* Watch for the miracle! See, she is moving her eyes!"

200

Under the pretext of wishing to adjust a candle burning before the image, I took a ladder and climbed until I was on a level with the face of the Madonna. I fixed the candle, but this was not the object of my climb. I wanted to observe minutely whether in the eyes of the effigy or around it there might be some cut or other mark which would excite suspicion—or perhaps something that would warrant seeking behind the painting an artificial means by which the eyes were moved. I was swiftly disabused of this idea, however, for I clearly saw that the painting, especially that section where the eyes were, was all smooth and without the slightest sign of artificiality or alteration.

On the following Monday a bold thought occurred to me. . . . I provided myself with a compass and made a visit to the shrine. I paused, reciting litanies and other prayers. About a quarter of an hour later the marvel took place before me. I hurriedly climbed the ladder, holding in my hands the compass I had prepared; once again I found myself on a level with the eyes of the effigy, and opportunely, for the pupils had not lowered but were still covered with the eyelids. I placed one point of the compass on the lower extremity of that part of the pupil which was not completely covered by the eyelid, and the other point of the compass I placed on the edge of the lower eyelid. By this scheme I hoped to see how much of the white portion could be seen. . . . When the pupil returned to its place I could no longer perceive any portion of the white since the pupil immediately adjoined the lower eyelid. I descended satisfied that I had done everything possible to verify the miracle and to exclude all the doubt that had been in my mind.

During these extraordinary events an eleven-year-old girl, Marianna Maronti, who had been a cripple from birth, was carried in the arms of her mother to the shrine. Hardly had she reached the sacred scene when the girl was instantly cured. Aroused to joy at the sight of this prodigy, the people again broke into cries of *"Evviva Maria!"*

After such marvels it was inevitable that devotion to this shrine became ever more popular. This in turn resulted in increased offerings which made possible plans for the great embellishment of the beloved place.

A royal devotee joined the number of those who have loved this *madonnella* when the English King James III, the Old Pretender, took residence in the adjacent Palazzo Savorelli, now called Palazzo Balestra. The monarch posted guards before the shrine so that the passageway leading to it might remain open all night.

Midway in the nineteenth century there arose around the humble shrine a sumptuous chapel. This was due to the generosity of the Papazzurri-Savorelli, the same family which had originally sponsored the shrine. The Marchesi Alessandro and Caterina commissioned in 1851 the architect Virginio Vespignani to construct a small sanctuary. He built the chapel which we admire to this day. Vespignani created so beautiful a work of art that he boasted unashamedly of it. He would often bring his pupils to the chapel in order to instruct them in points of architecture. His modestly proportioned little temple has a grandeur that is the admiration of visitors, especially in the harmony of the total result, its gracefulness of detail and the richness of its ornamentation. The outside is extremely simple. The door is framed by Doric pillars, and above it is the crest of the Papazzurri family. Above this is a tablet with the inscription:

Mariae Dominae Nostrae
ALEXANDER MUTIUS DE PAPPACIURRIS MARCH.
ANTEA SAVORELLIUS COM.

No sooner does one pass the threshold than he is overwhelmed by the richness of his surroundings. Gold appears in profusion everywhere: in the cupola, the arches, and all the cornices. Yet its presence does not create a sense of heaviness; it serves rather to place in relief the elegance of the exquisitely detailed ornaments which enliven the sober neoclassical lines of the interior. The aisle brings one into a small *crociera* surmounted by a dome divided into highly decorated sections rich in gold. In the midst of all the paintings and sculptures there are reproduced Latin epigrams together with a crest of the Savorelli. On the side walls two niches form arches like small chapels, with four smaller niches containing statues of angels by the sculptor Luigi Simonetti. Other niches near the altar are adorned with statues of angels.

In the vault of the cupola are resplendent ornamentations surrounding a fresco of the Immaculate Conception, circled by verses from the Magnificat. Below are reproduced Wisdom, Prudence, Fortitude, and Innocence painted by the artist Brumidi.

Over the altar a background of malachite, lapis lazuli, and other costly stones sets off the golden carved frame of the miraculous image of the Madonna, the title, *Causa Nostrae Laetitiae*, being inscribed under the frame. The painting is almost square in form and reproduces a half-bust of the Virgin. The countenance is most beautiful, perfectly oval, and is illumined by the sweet expression of the eyes.

The dedication of the new sanctuary took place May 31, 1851. The solemn ceremonies were attended by

several cardinals, archbishops, bishops, and other illus-
trious personages. Fr. Facchini, S.J., addressed the huge
gathering.

From then until the sad day of 1870 Roman nobles
and common folk alike came in procession almost
every night to recite their prayers in the chapel of the
Madonna dell'Archetto. After 1870 the architect Francesco
Vespignani, son of Virginio, took care of the chapel for a
few years, but then it was abandoned for a time. In 1918 a
new society was formed, the *Primaria Società Cattolica
Promotrice di Buone Opere*, and its members assumed
responsibility for the preservation of the shrine and
its exquisite chapel. Each night they unite in goodly
numbers for regular prayers, and annually on the feast of
the Nativity of Mary a solemn celebration is held under
their auspices.

No more appropriate place could be chosen to end this
pilgrimage to the street shrines of Rome than the chapel
of the *Madonna dell'Archetto*, a truly Roman sanctuary,
fragrant with Roman flowers and redolent of Roman
prayers, where every day devout witness is borne to the
love for Mary of that city which dares claim her Son as its
First Citizen: ". . . Roma onde Cristo è Romano."[2]

Epilogue

This is the first opportunity we have, as a group, to honor the memory of our beloved Episcopal Chairman, the late Cardinal Wright, who was called to his eternal reward on Friday, August 10, of this past year [1979].

Subsequent to his untimely demise, numerous articles and editorials have appeared, both at home and abroad, eulogizing the brilliant and polyhedric career of this remarkable man. Some focused their attention on his diversified achievements as a priest, as a bishop, and later as a cardinal—both in the literary field and in the realm of the pastoral apostolate. Others noted his warm personality, his unaffected approachability, and, of course, his phenomenal resourcefulness as an entertainer, his rare ability when it came to witticism and sparkling repartee. One feature stressed by most commentators was the Cardinal's intrepid championing of doctrinal orthodoxy, his unconditional submission to the Magisterium of the Church, his unswerving loyalty and attachment to the Vicar of Christ on earth.

While all the encomiums already mentioned are, of course, richly deserved, nevertheless, the delineation remains incomplete without reference to the Cardinal's tender devotion to the Mother of God and his tireless efforts to promote a scholarly appreciation of her prominent role in the scheme of salvation. As members of the Mariological Society of America, we reflect with heartfelt gratitude on this particular facet of his life which, to my knowledge, has so far been passed over in silence by the media.

The Cardinal's close association with our Society dates back to its very beginning in 1949. Shortly after our first convention in Washington, D.C., he asked us if he could join our group, and we assured him that we would be highly honored with his membership. He then invited us to hold our second convention in Worcester, Massachusetts, the see to which he had just been appointed first bishop.[1] His words of welcome to our delegates on that occasion, and the tremendous enthusiasm he evidenced toward furthering the specific aims of our Society, gave us an initial but very tangible clue to what was to become a wholehearted and uninterrupted collaboration that lasted until his dying days.

It was he, for example, who on his own initiative made available two distinct monetary awards calculated to promote interest in sound Mariology through our Society. The first would be bestowed on a priest of our Society who had made a notable contribution to the field of Marian theology, mainly through his writings. The second would be presented to the three best essays on Mariology submitted by seminarians, as part of a national contest organized under the supervision of the Board of Directors.

In recognition of his zeal and his magnanimous gestures in our behalf, the Board of Directors, meeting on January 4, 1951, unanimously selected then Bishop Wright as Episcopal Chairman of our Society—a charge he fulfilled with distinction up to the day he left us.

At the convention held in Pittsburgh in 1961, coinciding with Bishop Wright's celebration of his Silver Jubilee as a priest, our Society presented him with a gold chalice of elaborate craftsmanship, made especially for him in Germany and exhibiting various engraved symbolisms which were of particular significance to him. Visibly moved, he assured us that this was, without any doubt, about the most magnificent gift he had ever received from anyone and that he would treasure it with all his heart.

During the first years of our activities, Bishop Wright not only attended our annual conventions (in fact, most of the board meetings, which in those days were held frequently) but he also addressed our group on several occasions, always awakening in his audience a greater eagerness to fathom the richness of Mary's privileges. In later years, however, owing to various pressing duties, he was prevented from attending our meetings, although he never failed to assure us of his continued interest and his fervent prayers for the success of all our undertakings.

That the Mariological Society of America will sorely miss this faithful patron and generous benefactor is, of course, something of an understatement. Those of us who were privileged to work closely with him through the years, and who were enriched by his friendship and by his magnetic personality, will always cherish his memory as an ennobling and uplifting inspiration. May Our Blessed Lady, whom he served so unsparingly in this life, obtain for him now the full measure of heavenly bliss he so richly deserved.

Mention was made earlier of the Cardinal's preoccupation with doctrinal orthodoxy, of his unequivocal adherence to the papal Magisterium. I could expand on that subject at considerable length, but I will refrain from doing so; it would take us too far afield. Nevertheless, allow me to recall only a couple of incidents which portray him at his characteristic best in this connection.

On one occasion, while discussing various articles in *The Wanderer* which deplored the anti-Magisterium attitude of many of our priests, even on matters Mariological, he commented with great sorrow: "To me it is obvious that the devil is on the loose and is having a field day, counting some of our theologians as his first victims."

On another occasion, while I was a guest at his residence, he kept me till the late hours of the night in a spirited discussion of the problem created by *dissenting* theologians—those who, as he put it, hide behind their conscience in order to justify their open rejection of the teaching of the Holy See on matters of faith and morals. His contention was that these misguided gentlemen were doing incalculable damage, especially to our seminarians. At one point he turned to me and said: "You know, Juniper, when I think of the harmful influence our young men are being exposed to in many of our seminaries today, I am frightened at what the Church in the future will look like—*really frightened*." I will never forget the expression of grief on his face as he uttered those words.

Perhaps a fitting way to bring these remarks to a close is by quoting the significant tribute which our Holy Father Pope John Paul II paid the Cardinal on August 15 of last year [1979].

> As a priest, as a bishop in the United States of America, as a cardinal in charge of an important department of the Roman Curia, he was always faithful to his motto: *Resonare Christum corde Romano*. That really sums up his whole life. In fact, Cardinal Wright was a secure voice which preached Our Lord with a fidelity and a directness which arose from a *sensus Ecclesiae* which was second nature to him.[2]

The Cardinal, you may be sure, would have been delighted to hear those last few words. They *do* "sum up his whole life."

Juniper B. Carol, O.F.M.

Abbreviations

ACW   *Ancient Christian Writers: The Works of the Fathers in Translation*, ed. J. Quasten et al. (Westminster, Md.: Newman Bookshop, 1946–).

CSEL   *Corpus Scriptorum Ecclesiasticorum Latinorum* (Vienna, 1866–).

PG   *Patrologia Graeca*, ed. J.P. Migne (Paris, 1857–66).

PL   *Patrologia Latina*, ed. J. P. Migne (Paris, 1844–64).

Notes

Tribute to Cardinal Wright

Pope John Paul II, "Angelus Message of 15 August . . . Tribute to Cardinal Wright", in *L'Osservatore Romano*, English ed. (Aug. 20, 1979): 1.

See also, "Giovanni Paolo II Ricorda il Cardinale Wright—Con una Solenne Cappella Papale in San Pietro", in *L'Osservatore Romano* (Sept. 24–25, 1979): 2.

Introduction

[1] Wright was a student at the Boston Latin School from 1923–27.

[2] Wright was born in Boston on July 18, 1909. He was ordained a priest in Rome on December 8, 1935. Ordained auxiliary to the Archbishop of Boston on June 30, 1947, he served in his native city until 1950. On March 7 of that year he was installed as the first bishop of Worcester, Massachusetts. In 1959, after nine years in Worcester, he was installed as Bishop of Pittsburgh, where he served from 1959 to 1969. On March 28, 1969, John Joseph Wright was elevated by Pope Paul VI to the cardinalate and transferred to Vatican City as Prefect of the Sacred Congregation for the Clergy. He served in that office for ten years until his death in Boston on August 10, 1979.

[3] Wright was the homilist for Father Manton's Golden Jubilee as a Redemptorist. He preached at the Eucharist in the basilica of Our Lady of Perpetual Help, the Mission Church, Boston, on June 23, 1974.

See Wright's preface to Father Manton's book, *Ten Responsible Minutes* (Huntington, Ind.: Our Sunday Visitor, 1978), 7.

[4] Cardinal William H. O'Connell, from 1906–44 Archbishop of Boston, died on April 22, 1944. Wright served as his secretary from 1943 until the Cardinal's death.

[5] In 1937, and again in 1938, Wright served the village of Lembras par Bergerac, Dordogne, France.

[6] R. Stephen Almagno, O.F.M., *Cardinal John Wright the Bibliophile* (Pittsburgh: Pittsburgh Bibliophiles, 1980).

[7] In his introduction to vol. 1 (*The Boston Years: 1939–1950*) of *Resonare Christum: A Selection from the Sermons, Addresses, and Papers of Cardinal John J. Wright*, Monsignor Edward G. Murray writes: "He first came to public attention when in his senior year, as leader of the Boston College debating team, he shone in a victory over Oxford University at Symphony Hall."

[8] St. Paulinus of Nola, *Carmen XVII* (*CSEL* 30, 93): "per te barbari discunt resonare Christum corde Romano placidamque casti vivere pacem."

P. G. Walsh, in his translation of *The Poems of St. Paulinus of Nola* (*ACW* 40, 112), renders the text as: "In this mute region of the world, the barbarians through your schooling learn to make Christ's name resound from Roman hearts, and to live in purity and tranquil peace."

One time in his student days, Wright came across this text; it impressed him deeply. He included it in his thesis and—when ordained bishop—selected it as his motto and included it in his coat of arms.

See John J. Wright, *National Patriotism in Papal Teaching* (Westminster, Md.: Newman Press, 1956), xii; idem, "Paulinus of Nola", in *Classica et Iberica*, a festschrift in honor of the Reverend Joseph M.-F. Marique, S.J., ed. P. T. Brannan, S.J. (Worcester, Mass.: Institute for Early Christian Iberian Studies, 1975), 417–25.

Cardinal Wright's personal coat of arms is composed of the shield and its charges, the motto beneath the shield, and the external trappings around the shield.

Arms: a cauldron in silver resting upon a fire, or rising from the fire, and an eagle of gold between two fleurs-de-lis. The Cardinal's arms are based upon those sometimes attributed to his patron saint, St. John the Evangelist, in allusion to the Roman tradition of St. John before the Latin Gate and the miraculous escape of the Saint from the cauldron of boiling oil prepared for him under the Emperor Domitian. The fleurs-de-lis are taken from the arms of the Archdiocese of Boston, where Wright was born and served as Auxiliary Bishop, before being named to the See of Worcester and subsequently to the Diocese of Pittsburgh. These fleurs-de-lis also appear frequently on arms associated with the name *Wright*.

The Cardinal's motto: The words *Resonare Christum* are from the passage in the writings of St. Paulinus of Nola given above. Wright's translation reads: "Through you the heathens of our world's un-heeded parts/Have learned *to echo Christ* with Roman hearts/And live a life of chaste and stable peace."

The external ornaments are composed of the scarlet pontifical hat with its fifteen scarlet tassels on each side, arranged in five rows, and the episcopal gold cross indicating his Sacred Congregation. These are the presently accepted heraldic trappings of a prelate of the rank of cardinal-bishop. Before 1870 the pontifical hat was worn at solemn cavalcades held in conjunction with papal functions. The color of the pontifical hat and the number and color of the tassels are signs of the rank of the prelate. This custom is preserved in ecclesiastical heraldry.

The arms were designed in 1947, after Wright was named an auxiliary to the Archbishop of Boston and titular bishop to the See of Tegea. These arms were designed by Dom William Wilfred Bayne, O.S.B., of the then Portsmouth Priory—now Portsmouth Abbey—in Portsmouth, Rhode Island.

The shield has a rose-red tint. The cauldron is, as mentioned, silver, with the eagle and the fleurs-de-lis of gold.

This description and explanation of Wright's coat of arms is based —with my additions and corrections—on the text published on page 12 of the booklet entitled: *The Pontifical Liturgy in Memory of John Cardinal Wright* (Pittsburgh: St. Paul Cathedral, Aug. 20, 1979).

[9] Donald W. Wuerl, "The White Train Travels to Lourdes", *L'Osservatore Romano*, English ed. (Aug. 24, 1972): 4–5 and 6; idem, "A Lourdes Story", *L'Osservatore Romano*, English ed. (Aug. 22, 1974): 4–5; Joseph E. Manton, *Give God Equal Time* (Huntington, Ind.: Our Sunday Visitor, 1977), 199–205.

Chapter I
Our Lady of the Snow

[1] *The Litany of Loreto*.

[2] Lionel Johnson, "Dark Angel", *The New Oxford Book of English Verse 1250–1950*, ed. Helen Gardner (New York: Oxford University Press, 1972), 808–809.

[3] *Missale Romanum*, "Sabbato Sancto—Exsultet".

Chapter II
Pastoral Letter on the
Dogma of the Assumption

   This pastoral letter was published in pamphlet form by the Diocese of Worcester and then in *American Ecclesiastical Review* 124 (Feb. 1951): 81–96.

   [1] The doctrine of the Assumption was formally defined by Pope Pius XII on November 1, 1950. Earlier that year, in January, Pope Pius XII divided the Diocese of Springfield, Massachusetts, and established a new diocese—the Diocese of Worcester, Massachusetts—for all the people living in Worcester County.

   [2] Monsignor John F. Gannon—whom Wright appointed as first chancellor of the Diocese of Worcester—writes: "in 1950 a residence for the home of the Bishop at 2 High Ridge Road, off Flagg Street in Worcester, was purchased. It is located on the west side of the city, which area up to the town line of Paxton during the past fifty years has been well filled with new homes and well-developed living sections. Friends from Bishop Wright's years in Boston, plus gifts of many generous people in the diocese, helped to furnish it. One of the features of this house is an exquisite small chapel. It is oak-paneled with beautiful stained-glass windows, a gift from special friends in Boston. It was from that chapel that for the *first time* the radio Mass each Sunday and a special Saturday night broadcast of the recitation of the rosary and of religious news were broadcast throughout Worcester County by radio station WTAG. It reached out into some other parts of Massachusetts and into some neighboring stations.

   "Bishop Wright usually celebrated the radio Mass and also the Saturday rosary. . . ." John F. Gannon, *Some Personal Recollections of the Early Years of the Diocese of Worcester 1950–1959 (pro manuscripto*, June 1, 1981), sec. D, 4–5.

   [3] Among the Cardinal's papers I have found a text entitled *Unpublished Description of Cardinal Wright's "Flat"*. On page 3, the text reads: "One room is full of photos and pictures of Pittsburgh, and in the living room there are reminders of the Pittsburgh Cathedral as well as of ancient Rome and Paestum, plus a set of the works of Cardinal Newman, with a bust of the English Cardinal from friends in Ireland and photos of Newman given to the Cardinal by the

Pittsburgh Oratory. Only in his personal study and bedroom (larger than in Worcester, smaller than in Pittsburgh) are there intimate reminders of home and family. 'When I open the door leading to these rooms, I identify myself with Rome and the work here', Wright claims, 'and when I close that door I sneak home for a few hours, home and back a few years to other times and places.' " The unpublished text was written by Michael Wilson, author, veteran Rome correspondent, and Wright's close friend.

In his bedroom, I remember seeing a picture of his parents: John J. Wright (d. Aug. 28, 1962) and Harriet Cokley Wright (d. Dec. 28, 1969).

As Monsignor Edward G. Murray notes in his introduction to vol. 1 (*The Boston Years: 1939–1950*) of *Resonare Christum: A Selection from the Sermons, Addresses, and Papers of Cardinal John J. Wright*, Wright was very devoted to his parents. "His parents", writes Murray, "were the salt of the earth. And his mother, in particular, had a dynamism which he inherited."

At the time of Mrs. Wright's death, Eleanor Roberts wrote the following in the *Boston Herald Traveler*:

"Whenever anyone asked Cardinal John Wright's mother the obvious question: 'Aren't you proud of your son?' she had but one answer.

" 'Which son?' Mrs. Wright, who died yesterday, would ask in all seriousness.

" 'We were all equal in her eyes', the Cardinal told me in Rome last May. 'That's what made her such a wonderful mother. She loved each child for himself.'

"The Cardinal's favorite story about his mother goes back to the time of her audience with Pope Pius XII when he said to her, 'You must be very proud of your son.'

" 'She held out her charm bracelet to him—each medallion on it inscribed with the names of her children and grandchildren—and told him in detail about each one starting with, "My son, the doctor" ', the Cardinal said. The Cardinal has three brothers, Richard H. of Cleveland, Dr. Richard Wright of Milton, and Alfred of Dedham.

"The Cardinal in personality is very much like his mother, forceful and dynamic.

"Known as 'Hattie' to most of her friends, Mrs. Wright was the kind of mother who expected the most of her children—and got it.

"She was the soul of orderliness. Once this writer evoked her wrath when she mentioned in a feature story on her son John's elevation to Bishop of Pittsburgh that his desk was 'cluttered'.

" 'You're in the doghouse with my mother', the Cardinal reported the following morning. 'She wanted to know how you'd dare to say such a thing when she brought up all her children to be orderly and neat', he chuckled.

"No generation gap ever existed in the Wright home. 'We related very well. Mother was very purposeful and she communicated this to us', the Cardinal said.

" 'She always knew what interested each of us. She always had time to listen and to make a point of trying to understand, even when my brother Dick came home from medical school and discussed technical things with her.'

"Although it was a source of pain to each of her children to see their dynamic mother lie so seriously ill at Marian Manor in South Boston for the past one and a half years, they were all grateful she was fully aware that her son John had been elevated to the cardinalate.

" 'I told my mother, and I knew I got through to her', the Cardinal said on the flight to Rome. 'We were gathered at her bedside, and she looked up at us and said, "You're all going to Rome." It made me very happy.'

" 'We're all so grateful for the wonderful care my mother received from the Carmelite nuns at Marian Manor', his brother Alfred said last night. 'Sister Victoria, who took special care of Mother, was so dedicated—everything she did was special.'

"Now the boy who took those long walks with his mother and was so devoted to her will celebrate her funeral Mass on Wednesday morning." Eleanor Roberts, "Mrs. Wright Dead at 87", *Boston Herald Traveler* (Dec. 29, 1969): 1 and 8.

4 Valentine A. Mitchel, S.M., *The Mariology of Saint John Damascene* (Kirkwood, Mo.: Maryhurst Normal Press, 1930), 138–68; St. John Damascene, *Homiliae in Dormitionem Beatae Virginis Mariae* (*PG* 96, 699–762).

5 St. Augustine *De Natura et Gratia* (*PL* 44, 267).

6 Job 19:25–26.

7 Lk 1:49.

8 *The Litany of Loreto*.

9 Mt 2:11.

10 Jn 19:25.

218

[11] Samuel Eliot Morison, *The European Discovery of America A.D. 1492–1616* (New York: Oxford University Press, 1974), 53.

Chapter III
Mariology in the English-Speaking World

This paper was published in *Marian Studies* 2 (1951): 11–26.

[1] Alfred Noyes, ed., *The Golden Book of Catholic Poetry* (Philadelphia: J. B. Lippincott, 1946), 25.

[2] Ibid., 23–24.

[3] John Henry Newman, *Apologia* (London: Longmans, Green, 1921), 53 and 195.

[4] Among the Cardinal's papers I have found a text entitled *Unpublished Description of Cardinal Wright's "Flat"*. See chap. 2, note 3 above.

[5] Francis J. Friedel, *The Mariology of Cardinal Newman* (New York: Benziger, 1929), 1–142.

On page 14 of the printed text (*Marian Studies* 2 [1951]: 11–26) Wright wrote: "The indebtedness of the present paper to Father Friedel's book is complete and candid."

[6] John Henry Newman, *Parochial and Plain Sermons* (London: Longmans, Green, 1918), vol. 2, 135.

[7] John Henry Newman, *Discourses Addressed to Mixed Congregations* (London: Longmans, Green, 1899), 357–58.

[8] John Henry Newman, *Sermons*, vol. 2, 32, quoted by Friedel, op. cit., 155.

[9] Newman, *Sermons*, vol. 8, 252 and vol. 6, 314, quoted by Friedel, op. cit., 155.

[10] Newman, *Sermons*, vol. 2, 128, quoted by Friedel, op. cit., 155.

[11] Newman, *Sermons*, vol. 8, 233 and vol. 3, 128 and 131, quoted by Friedel, op. cit., 154–55.

[12] John Henry Newman, *Meditations and Devotions* (London: Longmans, Green, 1914), 38–39.

[13] Friedel, *The Mariology of Cardinal Newman*, 156.

[14] John Henry Newman, *Difficulties of Anglicans* (London: Longmans, Green, 1900), vol. 2, 62.

[15] H. Denzinger, *Enchiridion Symbolorum et Definitionum* (Fribourg, 1914), 113.

[16] Ibid., 148.

John Henry Newman, *Development of Christian Doctrine* (London: Longmans, Green, 1920), 310.

[18] Friedel, *The Mariology of Cardinal Newman*, 156.

[19] Newman, *Discourses*, 347.

[20] Ibid., 348; idem, *Development*, 426; idem, *Meditations and Devotions*, 69.

[21] Newman, *Discourses*, 349.

[22] *Breviarium Romanum*, Commune Festorum Beatae Mariae Virginis. In III Nocturno. I Ant.

[23] *PG* 94, 1029.

[24] Gen 3:20.

[25] Newman, *Difficulties*, 32.

[26] Gen 3:15.

[27] Newman, *Development*, 415; idem, *Meditations and Devotions*, 35; idem, *Difficulties*, 35.

[28] Newman, *Meditations and Devotions*, 36.

[29] Lk 1:38.

[30] Edward B. Pusey, *An Eirenicon, in a Letter to the Author of the "Christian Year"* (Oxford, 1865), 155–56 and 151.

[31] Newman, *Sermons*, 128–31.

[32] Newman, *Difficulties*, 36.

[33] *PL* 67, 1048.

[34] *PL* 40, 397 and 399.

[35] Newman, *Meditations and Devotions*, 64.

[36] Ibid., 66–67.

[37] Newman, *Difficulties*, 73.

Chapter IV
Lourdes, Land of the Rosary

This address was published in *Sign* 35 (Oct. 1954): 52–53, 76. Italian trans. in *L'Ancora* 22 (Aug. 1971): 5–10.

Chapter V
Mary Immaculate
Patroness of the United States

This article was published in *Thomist* 17 (Oct. 1954): 428–32.

[1] Hugh J. Nolan, ed., *Pastoral Letters of the American Hierarchy 1792–1970* (Huntington, Ind.: Our Sunday Visitor, 1971), 119 and 136.

² Daniel Sargent, *Our Land and Our Lady* (New York: Longmans, Green, 1939), 187.

Chapter VI
Mary and Modern Times

This article was published in *Annals of St. Anthony's Shrine* 10 (1955): 11–19.

¹ Lk 12:32.

Chapter VII
Our Lady of Space

This article was published in *Marist Missions* 14 (July–Aug. 1958): 15–18; *Our Lady's Digest* 13 (Jan. 1959): 233–37; *Marian Era* 3 (1962): 38–39.

¹ Ps 23:1.
² Ps 8.
³ *The Litany of Loreto*.
⁴ *Breviarium Romanum*, Commune Festorum Beatae Mariae Virginis. Ad I Vesperas. Hymnus. "Ave, Maris Stella."
⁵ Rev 12:1.
⁶ Prov 8:22–31.

Chapter VIII
Mary and Christian Unity

This sermon was published in *Catholic Mind* 58 (Dec. 1960): 566–69; *Marianist* (Jan. 1960): 4–8; *Annals of St. Anthony's Shrine* 15 (1960): 11–16.

¹ Jn 1:12–13.

Chapter IX
The Third Word from the Cross

In his introduction to *Words in Pain*, Wright stated: "These conferences were first preached at St. Clement's Shrine, Boston, in the Three Hours Devotion. They were subsequently repeated in the Cathedral of the Holy Cross and St. James Church, Boston, at other

Good Friday services. In their revised form, as here presented, they were preached in St. Paul's Cathedral, Worcester, Good Friday 1952, and as a Lenten course at St. Paul's Cathedral, Pittsburgh, 1960."

This conference was published in Bishop John Wright, *Words in Pain: Conferences on the Seven Last Words of Christ* (Notre Dame, Ind.: Fides, 1961), 39–47; French trans., *Paroles dans la souffrance: Les Sept Paroles du Christ*, trans. Louis de Corbiac (Montreal and Paris: Fides, 1963), 37–48. In the "Note de l'auteur", Wright stated: "La présente traduction a été réalisée avec une grande dévotion par le colonel Louis de Corbiac, autrefois maire de Lembras en Dordogne [France]. Jeune prêtre, alors que je desservais la paroisse du village, j'ai eu le privilège de demeurer dans cette famille profondément chrétienne." Italian trans., *Parole nella Sofferenza: Le Sette Parole di Cristo in Croce*, trans. Massimo Giustetti (Fossano: Editrice Esperienze, 1972), 37–44. Second English ed., *Words in Pain: Meditations on the Last Words of Jesus* (Notre Dame, Ind.: Ave Maria Press, 1978), 37–43.

[1] Jn 19:25–27.
[2] Lk 23:24.
[4] 2 Macc 7:20.
[5] Jn 19:25–26.

Chapter X
Our Lady of Guadalupe

This message was published in *Marianist* (June 1961): 2; *Marian Studies* 12 (1961): 5–7.

[1] Wright was ordained a priest by Cardinal Francesco Marchetti-Selvaggiani in Rome on December 8, 1935.

[2] Samuel Eliot Morison, *The European Discovery of America A.D. 1492–1616* (New York: Oxford University Press, 1974), 53.

Chapter XI
Eve, Mary, and the Modern Woman

[1] Beginning in 1948 Wright was the Episcopal Moderator of the National Retreat Movement for the Laity. See C. Hennessy, S.J., *The Inner Crusade: The Closed Retreat in the United States* (Chicago: Loyola University Press, 1965), v–vi, 156–57, 162–63, and 167–68.

While Bishop of Worcester, Wright founded the Lancaster Cenacle. Mother Helen M. Lynch, a Religious of the Cenacle, writes: "In June 1953, a new Cenacle was added to the growing number of foundations with the purchase of the former country estate of the late Bayard Thayer in Lancaster, Massachusetts. This foundation was the direct result of long importuning, as His Excellency, the Most Reverend John J. Wright, D.D., had ardently desired a retreat house for women since his consecration in 1950. For many years he had been closely associated with the Cenacle of Boston in its apostolate, and, as Episcopal Advisor of the National Retreat Movement, he now exercises indefatigable zeal in increasing retreat consciousness and retreat centers across the land." Helen M. Lynch, *In the Shadow of Our Lady of the Cenacle* (New York: Paulist Press, 1954), 247. See also Wright's prefatory note to *Women of the Cenacle* (Milwaukee: Convent of Our Lady of the Cenacle, 1952), ix–xi.

On April 13, 1959, less than a month after becoming Bishop of Pittsburgh, Wright wrote to Mother Gertrude M. Coleman: "When may I hope—or even may I hope?—to have a Cenacle in Pittsburgh? I beg you to include us on your list of *futurabilia* and to let me know whether I may not begin to look about for at least eventual places suitable for the supremely important work of the Cenacle."

But, because of Cenacle foundations in Florida and Lima, Peru, in the early 1960s, Pittsburgh did not get its Cenacle until the summer of 1965.

A press release, issued by Monsignor Daniel H. Brennan on June 19, 1965, stated: "Bishop Wright, at a business meeting of the Diocesan Council of Catholic Women (Saturday, June 19, 1965), announced the establishment here of a retreat house of the Religious of the Cenacle to be located on Fifth Avenue at Clyde Street in Oakland, on property formerly occupied by the Winchester-Thurston School.

"Bishop Wright's interest in the Order and its work has been both personal and official. During his days as a student priest in Rome he frequently offered Mass in the Catacomb of St. Priscilla, which is connected with the Cenacle convent in Rome, and later gave weekend retreats at the Cenacle convent in Brighton, Massachusetts. In 1953, as the first bishop of the Diocese of Worcester, Massachusetts, he introduced the Order into the new diocese at Lancaster, Massachusetts.

"Expressing his deep admiration for the Order in his prefatory note to the book *Women of the Cenacle*, Bishop Wright wrote: 'Any bishop whose heart burns with even a small part of St. Paul's solicitude for the Church would welcome in his diocese these spiritual coadjutors [the Cenacle sisters], so like those devout women of apostolic days in Rome whose households were places of prayer and spiritual refreshment for the Christian laity.'

"During the last two sessions of Vatican Council II, Bishop Wright had made the Cenacle motherhouse in Rome his headquarters and as Episcopal Moderator of the lay retreat movement in the United States keeps close contact with the Cenacle in this country."

2 Lk 1:38.

3 Lk 1:38.

4 Mt 5:48.

Chapter XII
The Cult of Mary in
The Age of the Cult of the Flesh

This sermon was published in *The Church: Hope of the World*, ed. Donald W. Wuerl (Kenosha, Wis.: Prow Books, 1972), 142–51; *L'Osservatore Romano*, English ed. (May 20, 1976): 6–7.

1 Lionel Johnson, "Dark Angel", *The New Oxford Book of English Verse 1250–1950*, ed. Helen Gardner (New York: Oxford University Press, 1972), 808–809.

2 *The Litany of Loreto*.

3 Jn 1:14.

4 St. Ignatius, *To the Ephesians* (*ACW* 1, 63).

5 St. Ignatius, *To the Smyrnaeans* (*ACW* 1, 93).

6 *Liturgia Horarum*, "Te Deum".

7 1 Cor 7:17.

8 1 Tim 4:1–5.

Chapter XIII
Mary, the New Eve

This sermon was published in *L'Osservatore Romano*, English ed. (Aug. 19, 1971): 4–5; *Our Lady's Digest* (Nov.–Dec. 1971): 117–26.

1 St. Ignatius, *Epistola ad Romanos* (*PG* 5, 686): "universo coetui charitatis praesidens."

[2] Jn 1:12–13.

[3] John Henry Newman, *Difficulties of Anglicans* (London: Longmans, Green, 1910), 31–33.

[4] Ibid., 36–37.

[5] Ibid., 40–41. Here, Wright has paraphrased Newman's text. The actual text reads: "She it is, who is signified by Eve, enigmatically receiving the appellation of the Mother of the living. It was a wonder that after the transgression she had this greatest epithet. And, according to what is maternal, from that Eve all the race of men on earth is generated. But thus in truth from Mary the Life itself was born in the world, that Mary might bear living things and become the Mother of living things. Therefore, enigmatically, Mary is called the Mother of living things. . . . Also, there is another thing to consider as to these women, and wonderful as to Eve and Mary. Eve became a cause of death to man . . . and Mary a cause of life; that life might be instead of death, life excluding death which came from the woman, viz., He Who through the Woman has become our life.—*Haer*. 78, 18."

Chapter XIV
Mary, Type of Servant And Agent of the Holy Spirit

This paper was published in *L'Osservatore Romano*, English ed. (June 19, 1975): 9–10.

[1] Ps 46:10.

[2] Lk 1:38.

[3] Wis 18:14–15.

[4] Lk 4:14–20.

[5] Lk 21:19.

[6] Ps 46:10.

Appendix
Some Street Shrines of Rome—I

This article was published in *American Ecclesiastical Review* 122 (Jan. 1950): 1–13.

[1] Chiesa Nuova (or S. Maria in Vallicella)—and its association with St. Philip Neri (his body rests in a chapel to the left of the high

altar), the Oratory, the Vallicella Library, and Cardinal Newman—was, of course, very dear to Wright.

In his introduction to vol. 2 (*The Pittsburgh Years: 1959–1969*) of *Resonare Christum: A Selection from the Sermons, Addresses, and Papers of Cardinal John J. Wright*, Bishop Anthony G. Bosco writes: "He introduced the Pittsburgh Oratory into the diocese. As a neighbor of the University of Pittsburgh, and loving academia as he did, John Wright was always interested in the university. He had a pastoral concern for the spiritual life and growth of the Catholic professors, students, and staff who frequented or worked at the university. So he entrusted this concern to the Fathers of the Oratory, the sons of St. Philip Neri and Cardinal John Henry Newman, with the hope that they would bring, as indeed they have, a new dimension to the Diocese of Pittsburgh." See John G. Deedy, Jr., "A First for Pittsburgh", *Information* 75 (Aug. 1961): 10–14. See also Raleigh Addington, *The Idea of the Oratory* (London: Burns and Oates, 1966), 95 and 130.

Appendix
Some Street Shrines of Rome—II

This article was published in *American Ecclesiastical Review* 122 (March 1950): 165–82. When this article appeared in print, the author had become the first bishop of Worcester. He was transferred from auxiliary to the Archbishop of Boston to the new See of Worcester on January 28, 1950, and enthroned on March 7, 1950.

[1] F. Marion Crawford, *Ave Roma Immortalis* (New York: Macmillan, 1898), vol. 1, 100–101.

[2] Wright was a student, and the vice-rector, of the North American College in Rome (at that time on the Via dell'Umiltà, near the Trevi Fountain). He was ordained there by Cardinal Francesco Marchetti-Selvaggiani on December 8, 1935. And he had a lifelong love affair with Rome, Italy, and things Italian.

In his introduction to vol. 2 (*The Pittsburgh Years: 1959–1969*) of *Resonare Christum: A Selection from the Sermons, Addresses, and Papers of Cardinal John J. Wright*, Bishop Anthony G. Bosco writes: "He loved the Vatican, the city of Rome, and the Italian people. He was one of the most *Italian Yankees* I have ever known. When I saw him in Italy or in one of the Italian churches of the Diocese of Pittsburgh, he would go native quite easily and naturally. He spoke some of the Italian dialects. He knew the songs and customs. He was very much at home. His Italian always had a New England, better, a Bostonian accent about it, but his heart was Italian through and through."

Appendix
Some Street Shrines of Rome—III

This article was published in *American Ecclesiastical Review* 122 (April 1950): 246–56.

[1] Wright was very fond of the santuario della Madonna del Divino Amore. As Father Manton noted in his introduction to this volume: "On Sunday afternoons [the Cardinal] loved to take a ride through the Roman countryside, eventually reaching some spot dedicated to the Madonna. More often than not his ride took him along the Appian Way to the shrine of *La Madonna del Divino Amore*."

[2] Dante, *Purgatorio*, bk. 32, 102: ". . . di quelle Roma onde Cristo è Romano."

Epilogue

This text was published as "Memorial Tribute to Cardinal John Wright", in *Marian Studies* 31 (1980): 36–39.

[1] Wright was installed as the first bishop of Worcester, Massachusetts, on March 7, 1950.

[2] Pope John Paul II, "Angelus Message of 15 August . . . Tribute to Cardinal Wright", in *L'Osservatore Romano*, English ed. (Aug. 20, 1979): 1.